A DOG'S LOVE

by
WILLIAM H. COX

Unless otherwise indicated, all scripture was taken from the King James Version of the Bible.

ISBN-13: 978-0692716366 (Rusty Iron Ranch, LLC)

ISBN-10: 069271636X

Other books written by William H. Cox
Skies Are Not Cloudy All Day – Is God trying to get your attention?

Available at website:
www.rustyironranchllc.com

Mail:
Rusty Iron Ranch, LLC.
P.O. Box 1582
Sandpoint, Idaho 83864

A DOG'S LOVE

WILLIAM H. COX

Preface

Dogs are amazing animals. We're blessed to share our daily lives with them. We connect with our dogs so easily because of their love and positive attitude. They work their way into our lives with ease, assuming their position in our families with their unconditional love. Dogs share many human traits and expressions that we cannot help but identify with. Through their example we can learn more about our relationship with God if we slow down our fast paced lives and observe them. It makes me wonder if that is what God had in mind when He created them. It seems that dogs are the perfect visual example of what He desires in a relationship with us. Adam even named them God spelled backwards possibly as a reflection of that unconditional love. The bible says that Adam walked in the cool of the day with the Lord before the fall of man. I believe that Adam knew God much better than we do because sin hadn't separated us from God yet. Maybe Adam noticed that correlation with these amazing animals and I have to imagine that God hopes that we would grasp that understanding as well.

A Dog's Love is a compilation of how God has used two cow dogs and my friend's Dachshund in my life to reveal His love and character to me. I think He sent us these loyal and devoted animals as companions in the hopes that we could embrace the humble childlike love that flows out of them and as an example of how we should approach Him. After reading this book, I hope the correlation that we have with our loving Father through these loving animals is evident.

That being said, I believe in order to truly know God and have a relationship with Him we need to personally invite Him into our hearts, repent from sin that we all have within us and diligently study His word to see His true character. I have provided scriptures from the Bible at the end of each chapter to help show the reflection and similarities of the relationship we have with God and dogs through these short stories.

To clarify, God is beyond measure the ultimate, "Man's best friend"! Nothing truly can compare to Him and His love for us. He is Holy and Almighty.

I hope this book will bless you and make you see how much your Heavenly Father loves you!

Dedicated to my friend Karen.

*Now unto him that is able to do exceeding
abundantly above all that we ask or think,
according to the power that worketh in us, Unto
him be glory in the church by Christ Jesus
throughout all ages, world without end. Amen*

Ephesians 3:20-21

8

The Dance

"You need a dog out there on the ranch with you!"
Aaron insisted.

I knew he was right, but I was still aching from the pain
of having to put Merl down several years before. He
had been a good dog and such a good friend. I felt like I
was almost cheating on my ole' buddy by even looking
at another dog.

After relentless prodding from Aaron I decided to at
least go look at Cowgirl. After all, she was the last one
available from the abandoned litter found in an old
horse trailer.

I justified getting her since I had been without a dog for
several years and recently moving out of the city. I
needed a dog to help on the ranch. Surely Merl would
understand that! I made a mental note not to allow this
new dog to wiggle its way into my heart like Merl had!

Packed full of energy and bouncing across the carpet in
her white socks, Cowgirl had two big, brown eyes that
absorbed everything around her. She was about ten
weeks old when I brought her home to the ranch. Her
tail revealed her temperament and went wild when her
eyes met mine. She was cute as a button but was in
desperate need of training. She had a terrible habit of
chewing on everything in sight. I don't know how she

avoided electrocution when she chewed through the wires on the television. And then there was the peeing on the floor. No matter how many times I swatted her on the butt, she could not grasp the concept. The problem was that after I swatted her butt, she avoided me and would not come when I called her.

One particular spring day after waking up to a giant wet spot in the middle of the living room carpet, the defining moment came. She was ruining the carpet and the house was beginning to smell. I grabbed her sternly, causing her to pee more and rubbed her nose in it while reprimanding her with a stern, "No!" Then I gave her a stiff spanking and sent her outside. I was getting fed up with her disobedience and every time I walked by her, I gave her a disapproving look. She responded by looking down ashamed.

Later that morning Jayme, a friend of mine, came over for a lunch date, and when I called Cowgirl, she wouldn't come to me. At first she was defiant and ignored me. I called to her sternly, and it was obvious that she was scared that she might get another spanking. She looked at me out of the corner of her eye and shifted around nervously with her back towards me then ran around the house out of sight. She had clearly gotten the message that I was upset with her all morning.

I told Jayme that she might as well go in the house and relax a while because this dog thing might take some time. I went back outside to Cowgirl and called her again walking towards her. First, she ran out by the haystack. I stopped, called again and she reluctantly came within twenty feet, stopped, turned back about three feet, and laid down away from me watching out of the corner of her eye. I insisted that she needed to come all of the way but quickly realized that was not going to happen. She didn't move. She feared that she would get another spanking now for disobeying. I felt terrible realizing how sensitive she was. I was going to have to change the way I punished her but still by the end of the day she *was* going to come to me, and we were going to get this whole thing worked out.

It was Saturday and there was a great deal of work to be done. Weeds were starting to come up and needed spraying, fields needed fertilizer, ditches needed burned, fences needed mending, calving was in progress, the irrigation system needed to be primed and pipes needed to be laid out and checked. The Cowgirl problem in the midst of all of these chores annoyed me, but I figured as smart as she was she would sense my annoyance.

With a surrendered sigh, I chose to change my demeanor and did my best not to show any impatience. I looked down at her and smiled. We were at a standoff; me at six feet, 230 pounds, and her maybe ten inches tall and five pounds dripping wet. Whenever I took a step towards her, she would move away a step. The farm was thirty acres so I figured we had plenty of room

11

to do this little dance, and it was *her* dance. We were going wherever she decided to go.

We went around the house and out of the yard through the gate, past the big, yellow, barn cat sunning herself and alongside the chicken pen. The cat watched lazily with one eye half open as we danced. Cowgirl was completely fixated on me and what I was doing, not even noticing the cat! The chickens were completely perplexed by the whole ordeal and stood at the wire mesh, heads cocked to one side, watching with great interest. Cowgirl went around the corner, past what was left of the haystack, alongside the corral and the chute, down the fence line along the alfalfa field, through the swale by the canal, and up across the back grass pasture one step at a time. The cows lined up like spectators along the edge of the fence watching this promenade with interest as I went forward and Cowgirl went backwards step by step. I was beginning to wonder if we were going to cross over into the Bureau of Land Management ground! How far was this little dog going to go?

When we reached the top of the hill at the very back fence, in the far corner of the property, I sensed that she was wearing down. Or maybe she sensed that I was and was willing to give me a break. I stopped and studied her patiently. Then, I knelt down on one knee and she laid down, her eyes never leaving me. I took my gaze off of her and watched the gentle breeze blow giant white puffy clouds across the sky. Their shadows raced across the field chasing after them, and when the clouds blocked the sun's warm rays over me, the temperature dropped nearly ten degrees. I was in a short sleeve t-shirt and the temperature change was uncomfortable in the shade. A meadowlark perched on a fencepost watched this fascinating ordeal unfold, occasionally letting go with his melodious sonnet to a suitor hidden in the tall grass.

I told Cowgirl ever so gently that she really needed to come to me and that life would be so much more rewarding when she did. When she heard her name her ears relaxed in response, and the little knob of a tail wiggled just a hair. I opened my hand and held it out to her. Her head went down still looking up at me, and she took a tiny step towards me then plopped down. I told her it was okay and we would stay out here all night if that is what it was going to take. Each time I spoke to her, she lowered her head sheepishly, took another step in my direction and plopped down.

This went on for some time and after a few minutes she was right next to me sitting upright and looking at me with her big, brown eyes. Her expression tore at my heart. How could anyone in their right mind get mad at this little dog? I gently slid my hand alongside her face, and she laid her head in my hand. I sat down and patted my thigh. Slowly, she crawled up into my lap. She sat there for a little bit looking at me out of the corner of her eye. I softly ran my hand up her back, telling her it was going to be alright. She released a quiet sigh and then with complete submission let go, falling onto my chest. Her nose nudged up towards my face and her tongue gently licked my neck and ear. I caressed the side of her face telling her that I was sorry for spanking her and explained that we had rules that we had to live by and those rules were for her overall safety and quality of life. If she would accept them and live by them, it would ultimately make life go a lot smoother for both of us.

After a bit I laid back in the tall grass with her on my chest. I watched her long, black hair stir as the breeze picked up, and her ears twitched in different directions at sounds that only she could hear. Intriguing scents from faraway lands hit her nostrils which caused her little nose to quiver in a frenzy as she tested each one carefully. I thanked God for giving me this little dog. The meadowlark called again, and I thought about all of the work that needed to be done. Then I remembered Jayme was back at the house. I gave Cowgirl a kiss and a pat on the head as I got up to head back. She looked up at me as her butt wiggled. As we started to walk, she ran circles around me, barking and gently grabbing the cuffs of my Levi's in her teeth, growling dramatically. She was happy for my forgiveness and delighted to be back in good standing with me. The gift of forgiveness was just that - a precious gift!

As we were walking back to the house, I thought about the times when God spoke to me about forgiveness. Many of those times I wouldn't budge and even ran from God. But forgiveness is a big deal! The Bible teaches us in Ephesians 4:26,, "let not the sun go down on your wrath," if left unattended, unforgiveness can actually become debilitating. Not practicing forgiveness can turn into bitterness which has many side effects like depression, anger, loneliness, and sadness.

There will be people in life who will do things that are unjust. We will always have to deal with others and being human, we all fall short at one point or another. It's a messy thing, but eventually someone is going to get hurt.

Unresolved forgiveness and conflict interrupts our prayer life which is our direct communication line with the Lord. This interruption makes us ineffective in spiritual battles that are constantly going on around us. Satan knows this and will try to use it.

The disciple Peter came to Jesus and asked Him how many times we should forgive someone. Is seven times enough? Jesus' reply was "seventy times seven" or in other words, we should *always forgive*.

When God sees us forgive someone the same way He forgives us, it brings Him great pleasure, just like Cowgirl and me. Picture Him looking at you sitting on His lap. He is proud of you and loves you!

Reconciliation's reward is a sweet and carefree life! The warm breeze blowing through our hair feels good and

without that extra burden, we can enjoy this life more
freely.

A Bone to Chew On:

Have you ever run from God because you were
ashamed of what you had done, or maybe you didn't
want to do what He asked you to do?

Has God ever come after you when you ran from Him?

Do you need to forgive someone who has hurt you?

Have you done something to someone that you need to
ask forgiveness for?

Do you have any pain or hurt that has turned to anger
or bitterness in your life?

Ephesians 4:26 *"Be ye angry, and sin not: let not the sun go down upon your wrath"*

Proverbs 3:11-12 *"My son, **despise not the chastening of the LORD; neither be weary of his correction, For whom the LORD loveth he correcteth**; even as a father the son in whom he delighteth."*

Mathew 5:23 *"Therefore if thou bring thy gift to the altar, and there rememberest that thy brother hath ought against thee; Leave there thy gift before the altar, and go thy way; **first be reconciled to thy brother, and then come and offer thy gift.**"*

Matthew 18:22 *"Then came Peter to him, and said, Lord, how oft shall my brother sin against me, and I forgive him? till seven times? Jesus saith unto him, **I say not unto thee, Until seven times: but, Until seventy times seven.**"*

Teamwork

Every year my neighbor, Rick, and I pooled our money
together and bought a bull for breeding both of our
herds. After the bull was finished, we would sell it with
hopes of making a little money or at least breaking
even. This particular year we bought a Black Angus bull.
He was a large pureblooded, registered Angus. Rick told
me that we were fortunate to get such a screaming deal
on him. The previous owner had bottle fed him from a
calf and assured Rick that the bull's temperament was
good around his family. The bull had chased the rancher
only once in the field. He said they had children at
home and the chasing incident had been just a "one
time" deal, but as cheap as they were selling him I had
to wonder. Rick made all the arrangements and as it
worked out, I took the bull first to breed my cows, and
then we moved the bull over to his ranch to breed his
cows. Rick happened to tell me all of this just after they
delivered Herbie.

It was on a Sunday night around 7:00 p.m. in the
evening. We backed the stock trailer to the gate and
opened it into the pasture. Herbie didn't need any
coaxing. He exited the trailer in an air born gallop
leaving it rocking back and forth on the tandem axels
quite dramatically. Herbie assumed the role of "King",
quickly and ran out into the field head held high,
scouring the pasture for his harem to conquest. He

knew exactly what his job was and was eager to get to it. Spotting the cows in the far corner, he galloped full speed to where they were grazing. They saw him coming and hysteria ensued. He circled each one aggressively, checking to see if any were in heat by smelling under their tails and curling up his nose. The cows milled around excitedly with the new addition to the herd. Newborn calves moved quickly off to the side of the herd and away from the aggressive activity. A yearling steer who had previously assumed the leadership position challenged Herbie and a shoving match began. It didn't take long before the large bull had knocked the steer down and rolled him over in the dust. Humiliation came quickly as the steer got up and regained his composure with a newly acquired respect for the newcomer on the place.

There was a two-year-old heifer that had come into heat the day before, and although she thought that this big ole' boy who had come to visit was pretty darn exciting, she didn't understand why he was so aggressively jumping on her back. Her confusion was obvious. *Out of all these girls in the pasture, why is he riding my back?* She took off trying to elude him and the whole herd took off running erratically after her. Herbie had his sights locked in on this pretty, little heifer and she was not going to get away!

After much circling, he wore her down and cornered her in the back of the property along the fence by the canal. Again he tried mounting her. Shocked, she shot like a bottle rocket clearing the fence with room to spare. Instinctively, he followed right after her. Off they went down the canal bank headed to parts unknown to either one of them. It was like a true western with dust trailing behind them as they galloped off into the sunset. The remainder of the herd stood at the fence in awe like they were watching the credits roll on the latest chick flick that had ended too soon. By the way the herd pressed the fence, I figured some of them planned on joining the party.

The reality of it for me was like watching $3,000 blow down the canal road. To add greater misery they were both black, and it was about to get dark. This had the potential to get ugly in a hurry!

For Cowgirl and I, who were exhausted having just finished irrigating the alfalfa field, it was like watching the beginning of a horror story. I pulled my irrigation boots back on, grabbed a whip and headed for the truck. We drove about half a mile down the county road and then cut back over to the canal road to head them off.

The side of the canal they were on was actually an easement for the ditch company but was rarely used to drive on. It had been recently disked for weed control and spring burning so it was very soft and dusty. The loose dirt was difficult to drive in. Slipping the truck into four wheel drive, I hoped that we wouldn't get stuck, which would potentially end in greater disaster for me than for the poor pursued heifer.

As we pulled up blocking their path, I could tell that the heifer was stressed and feeling cornered. The way she was acting, I could tell that she seriously debated crossing the canal. The one thing hindering her decision was that the canal was full of swift moving water. The Black Canyon Ditch Company who had disked the canal road had also cleaned the ditch out earlier that spring, leaving the canal banks very steep.

My neighbor, Bad Bob, had a donkey that slipped into the canal a few weeks before, and it took several neighbors and a tractor most of the afternoon to get the animal out. And, that was in the daylight! The bleak thought crossed my mind, and I did not want to imagine the scenario of trying to get a love-struck bull and a frantic heifer out of the canal and back into the pasture, especially in the middle of the night! I started praying, *"Lord! PLEASE! I need your help NOW!!!"*

My heart hit the bottom of my stomach when the bull wheeled and turned towards me, blowing snot. His huge head lowered and his giant hoof dug up the loose dirt and flipped it into the air over the top of his back and across the hood of the truck. Dust filled the air, but he had made it quite clear that I was infringing on his domain, and he was ready to take on anyone who was planning to interfere. The thought of him flipping me,

Cowgirl and the truck over into the canal tumbling downstream made me nauseous.

Various scenarios raced through my mind when the heifer decided to turn and headed back down the canal towards more familiar territory and the beckoning calls of her herd.

The standoff with the bull seemed to last forever until he realized that she was no longer next to him and Herbie turned in hot pursuit after her. Hearing him on her heels, she broke out in a gallop, jumped the fence back into the field to the safety of the herd with him right behind her. However, Herbie didn't bother jumping the fence but plowed right through it, breaking off the wooden fence post at the brace and tearing out thirty yards of barbed wire and t-posts. Both the hot and barbed wires were now broken and laid in the field, in loose coils. Great! Now I had to get them out of that pasture and into the adjoining one because I didn't have time to fix fence that night! It was pushing 9:30 p.m., the sun had set, and I needed to be up at 4:00 a.m. the next day to change water before heading into town to work.

The cows were quite excited to have the elopers back in the pasture, and they were all bucking around in frenzied excitement. The young calves were running around in confusion trying to keep up with their mothers. Some of them had just given up and were standing off to the side taking it in. The bull was still concerned about me and had squared off just inside the fence, defending his newly acquired harem. Herbie had trashed the fence, and it now lay wide open. It wouldn't take much for one of the yearling steers running around half-crazed to see the opening and the whole herd would be out!

All of this excitement was affecting Cowgirl, too. She whined and looked up at me, begging me to let her go after the bull. Cowgirl was only nine or ten months old, and I had never let her go after a cow yet. I had practiced with her on the chickens, and she had done okay. She seemed to listen well, but I was still a bit reluctant, especially being so close to dark. Something needed to be done soon because the bull wouldn't budge and the cows were excited! The thought of all of the possibilities made me anxious. She was proving to be one of the best dogs I ever had, and not just a working dog but a dear companion too. I didn't want her getting kicked in the head on top of everything thing else.

I grabbed Cowgirl's collar and looked her square in the eyes and said, "Okay, now listen to me . . . *Pay attention!*"

I opened the truck door and we both got out. She was ready to go but she hesitatingly looked up at me. "Good girl," I said. "Okay, *go get him!*"

24

A black streak headed at the bull and lunged in the air, body slamming right into his neck! She was growling loudly, which got everyone's attention!

I said under my breath, "Wow, girl! Take it easy on the steak!"

The bull was not ready for that brutal attack, and the combination of shock and percussion nearly knocked him over! The cows stood in shock and awe as well, resulting in pandemonium. They took off in a frenzied gallop up the hill with their tails high in the air. The terror attack that had been unleashed upon them was new, and they wanted no part of it! The entire herd headed towards the gate at the top of the hill, which was open into the neighboring pasture. Halfway up the hill a handful of yearlings veered off to the right, attempted to cut down away and bypassed their escape route. I whistled and Cowgirl turned to look at me. I pointed at them, and she responded immediately, turning them back in the right direction. Another group of calves cut back to the left and I yelled, "Hey!" Pointing in their direction, she was after them. In a matter of seconds she had all of them in the other pasture and was sitting at the gate's entrance, panting and on guard. The only hint of the terrified herd in that field was the lingering dust settling in around her. I panted too when I finally got to her and shut the gate. "What a good dog!" Her butt wiggled with delight when I praised her. I was darn proud of that little dog, and I let her know as we walked back to the truck, still parked on the canal road.

What a team! We worked well together. I saw the big picture and was able to relay that to Cowgirl, who only saw what was going on within a few feet around her through all of the dust.

In contrast, my friend, Steve, who lived in Montana, told me a story about a dog he had that didn't always come when he was called. His dog was a runner. As soon as his dog had an opportunity, he ran and was unlikely to return until he was completely exhausted.

One Sunday afternoon in August, Steve and his wife were picking huckleberries in the Tobacco Root Mountains. They let their dog out of the car, and as usual, he took off to parts unknown. Steve and his wife secured their buckets and headed out to find berries in the patch near their parked car. Before they were very far, they heard the dog barking and growling erratically in the distance. The noise sounded as though there was a fierce fight going on. Looking up to see what all the commotion was, Steve was startled to see his dog running back towards him with a black bear in hot pursuit! He yelled at his wife, who was further away but had witnessed the same show and she was promptly climbing a tree. My friend bee-lined it back to the car and dove in the open window, frantically rolling all the windows up. The bear followed the dog to the car, and Steve laid on the horn, eventually spooking the bear off.

However, the irritated bear left a dent on the hood of their Honda. Steve's equally irritated wife had scratches on the insides of her arms and legs from scrambling up a tree in shorts! I am not saying this couldn't have happened to any other dog, but it most likely wouldn't have occurred if their dog paid attention.

We plug along through life trying to make the best decisions we can. The problem with us is that we cannot see what is constantly trying to trip us up. The Bible says that the devil is like a roaring lion searching to destroy. We can't always see what is going on ahead of us, and that is why it is so important to have good communication with God. Communication is important in every relationship. God communicates with us through our prayers to Him; reading His Word, the Bible; and through other Christians. Learning to pay attention to God involves staying in the Word, praying, fasting and fellowship, which is so important.

When we seek God and don't hear from Him, it can be frustrating. We want Him to direct us right now, but we need to trust that He knows when the timing is perfect. When we wait patiently, everything will fall perfectly into place. The Bible says that if we acknowledge Him in all of our ways, He will direct our path. I spent many years with good-ole' me directing my paths, and I can say it sure goes a lot smoother with the *Lord telling me* which way to go! I learned to take my own medicine, like Cowgirl...*Pay Attention!*

A Bone to Chew On:

Do you feel sometimes like you are out ahead of God, running wild?

Do you wait for His instructions?

How would you rate your communication with God?

How often do you get on your knees when you talk to God?

Do you have specific time set aside to spend with Him every day?

How do you gauge what God is saying to you?

1 Peter 5:8 **Be sober, be vigilant; because your adversary the devil, as a roaring lion, walketh about, seeking whom he may devour**

Isaiah 55:8 "**For my thoughts are not your thoughts, neither are your ways my ways,** saith the LORD.."

Proverbs 3:5-6 *Trust in the LORD with all thine heart; and lean not unto thine own understanding.* **In all thy ways acknowledge him, and he shall direct thy paths**

Proverbs 23:26 "**My son, give me thine heart, and let thine eyes observe my ways.**"

It Stinks

A couple years ago Cowgirl and I arrived at the office in town for work. I worked for a landscape architect/engineering firm. The job required me to up my standards and dress nicely. Despite the dress code, nothing prevented Cowgirl from coming to work with me every day. If it got too hot or cold out in the truck, I kept a plastic kennel under the desk in my cubicle where she could stay.

We had a routine we went through every morning and had been consistent for seven years; it was instigated by a cat.

There was a feral cat that hung around the office, and one morning Cowgirl and the cat met each other. This cat was much more aggressive than the barn cats we had at the ranch. Cowgirl had the barn cats buffaloed but this city cat was a scrapper! One morning Cowgirl met the feral, city cat behind the dumpster; it was a meeting she wouldn't soon forget. What a commotion! The cat had been hiding kittens somewhere around the dumpsters and we all know how moms are with their little ones. She was on top of the concrete block wall surrounding the garbage dumpsters, humped up, hair standing straight out in every direction, and yowling, which got Cowgirl really excited! The screeching and yowling was amplified even louder as it echoed off the surrounding buildings, completely shattering the still

31

morning air. There was so much racket it was almost embarrassing, and I was so thankful that I was the first one to work that morning!

Each morning after the feral cat event, Cowgirl headed back to the shrubs that surrounded the block walls and the dumpsters. The cat was wise and after the initial encounter, she made herself and her family scarce. Cowgirl, being the eternal optimist, never forgot and each day hoped that this was the day they would finally finish their fiasco!

One fall morning as I arrived to work as usual, I let Cowgirl out of the truck. I sensed in my gut that something wasn't right. Cowgirl had taken off on her mad dash to surprise the wily cat that wasn't there. I hobbled around to the other side of the truck. Due to a bad case of gout, everything I did that morning was painful. I had brought some extra vegetables from the garden for fellow employees and while making my way around the truck, I saw out of the corner of my eye some movement in the bushes, something black and white. It was early morning so I hadn't had my much-needed cup of coffee yet, so it took a minute for everything to compute. When it all came together, I yelled, "Whoa!" At the same time I heard a whimper and looked to see Cowgirl in sudden shock getting the blast from the skunk right in the face.

In no time the smell was everywhere and it was *intense*. Cowgirl turned and stumbled her way back to me, blinking her eyes, sneezing profusely and foaming at the mouth. All she wanted to do was crawl up in my lap, and I did not want her anywhere close to me. The problem was I couldn't quit laughing, and with my bad case of gout, I couldn't get away from her fast enough. She brushed up against my leg while I was trying to load her in the back of the truck. By now the smell had permeated the entire business complex, so much so that when Misty, the secretary, came into the office she began dry heaving! And I was guilty of stink by association. I thought it was a bit presumptuous for Misty to know that I was the root cause of all the stink!

Without traveling all the way back to the ranch to change clothes, I decided to keep my doctor's appointment because I had to get some relief from my gout. I had time to wait until the doctor's office opened so decided to get some work accomplished while waiting. Misty informed me that I needed to leave because the office was quickly becoming unbearable. Her attempt to open all of the doors was not helping the situation either! The stink was much worse outside. As people arrived to work, it quickly became unanimous that Cowgirl and I needed to go to the doctor's office to wait.

The receptionist was polite enough when I checked into the doctor's office. I couldn't help but notice that she closed the sliding glass door between her desk and the waiting room. I was sure that had nothing to do with me, but I did notice a group of nurses gathered behind the glass window were laughing and waving frantically. One nurse even went so far as to dramatically plug her nose and walked to a back office. There was no one in the office when I arrived so I enjoyed the solitude while reading a magazine. I attempted to situate myself in a far-away corner but still noticed a lingering odor that I hoped no one would notice.

When I heard the door open, a young man walked by and looked at me with a sideway glance and wrinkled his nose. I was hiding behind the magazine pretending not to notice the reaction. A few more people came in and the seats furthest from me were occupied forcing them to sit closer to me. One lady gave me a terrible look and I mumbled, "Sorry," making the least amount of eye contact that I could. She got up and went over to the lady behind the glass. I could tell they were talking about me. Then a lady walked by with her three year old daughter. That little girl was obviously sick but when she looked at me, she gave me the true definitive expression of "Stink Eye". It was clear that I repulsed her! It was like I had stink clinging all over me. I tried to explain that it was my dog who got tangled up with the skunk not me, but it didn't matter. I was guilty because it was on me too! They looked at me pathetically with their noses turned up. I disgusted them! I wanted to leave but a forty-five-mile commute back to the ranch was not a trip I wanted to make just to change clothes, and I really needed the medication to relieve the pain in my foot.

I was glad when they finally called my name. The doctor was young and had a good sense of humor. Apparently he had already gotten wind that I was the cause of adversity in the waiting room. In order for his business to thrive that day, he knew I needed to be seen, helped immediately and dismissed. The visit was short, and he offered me a remedy for quick removal of the stench, an added bonus.

He explained that when he was in chemistry during college, one of their assignments was to make a mixture of various chemicals to create the smell of a skunk and then neutralize the smell by adding the right chemical compound. He told me to get tomato juice, vinegar and hydrogen peroxide and mix it together. If I rubbed it into Cowgirl's hair, the smell of skunk would be instantly neutralized.

After my appointment, I stopped by the drugstore to get my medication filled as well as the mixture for Cowgirl and myself. In the parking lot, I mixed everything and took care of the problem! I couldn't believe how instantaneously it removed the stink. Immediately! I was amazed and so thankful as was *everyone* at the office!

On the way home that afternoon, I thought of how fast the solution worked. One simple component changed everything. I considered how people's reaction towards Cowgirl and me had also changed. The more I thought about it, the tomato juice mixture was just like the blood of Christ that He shed on the cross. He wiped away all the stink of past sin in our life. Immediately. Once and for all. Forever. Even the stink by association!

A Bone to Chew On:

Have you ever been caught off guard by sin?

Do you have the essence of sin lingering on you?

Have you ever been guilty of something by association?

Do you think others see sin in your life clinging onto you?

Have you applied the cleansing blood of Jesus to remove sin?

Isaiah 1:18 *"Come now, and let us reason together, saith the LORD: though your sins be as scarlet, they shall be as white as snow; **though they be red like crimson, they shall be as wool.***"

Revelation 1:5 *And from Jesus Christ, who is the faithful witness, and the first begotten of the dead, and the prince of the kings of the earth. **Unto him that loved us, and washed us from our sins in his own blood,***

1 John 1:7-9 *But if we walk in the light, as he is in the light, we have fellowship one with another, and **the blood of Jesus Christ his Son cleanseth us from all sin.** If we say that we have no sin, we deceive ourselves, and the truth is not in us. **If we confess our sins, he is faithful and just to forgive us our sins, and to cleanse us from all unrighteousness.***

Burying Bones

During the summer, there never seemed to be enough time in the day. On the farm, I got up early and went to bed when I couldn't move anymore. A typical summer day began at 4:00 a.m. with chores, then into town to put in eight to ten hours at the office, and then back to toil on the farm until dark. Most folks think that is way too much work. For me, work on the farm wasn't really work as much as it was living. Being a bachelor, there were times during the summer when I thought about how great it would be to have a wife who wouldn't mind cooking dinner and helping out with some of the chores. Because I didn't have that luxury, I had to take the extra time to cook dinner or pick up something in town. That usually meant pizza. It was easy to cook and Cowgirl loved the pizza crust. On Saturdays during the summer, if we got our chores done before the pizza place closed, we celebrated by going into town and picked up a take-out pizza which I brought home and baked.

By the time we drove into town, picked up the pizza, cooked it and started eating it on the deck, the sun would be setting. I loved that time of evening. All of the hard work was worth that little period of time when we sat on the back porch and enjoyed the fruits of our labor. Cowgirl and I relaxed and watched the shadows stretch across the field while calves got rambunctious chasing each other in the pasture. Sorties of hawks flew back from their desert hunting excursions to roost in the trees around the neighboring farms. Gradually the skies grew a golden orange blending in with the brilliant blue shadows and a gentle breeze floated down the draws towards the river, giving a little relief from the brutally hot summer day.

Cowgirl sat right next to me staring intently at slices of pizza secretly hoping that if she focused hard enough, she would cause the pizza to be tossed prematurely towards her. She got so absorbed that eventually a little drool emerged from the corners of her mouth.

After she ate a couple of pieces, she got full and took the rest of them out to her secret hiding place to save for later. She didn't want anyone to see where she buried them, including me, so it was quite humorous to watch her go to great lengths to bury these crusts. She ran across the lawn, crawled under the pole fence and looked both directions. At first, she casually looked back out of the corner of her eye to see if I was watching her, not wanting to reveal that she was paying any attention to me. If she thought I wasn't watching, she buried them right there, but if she thought I was paying attention, she went on around behind the tree to hide them so I couldn't see.

On one such evening, two magpies showed up and sat in the tree in front of the house. Somehow they knew it was *Saturday Pizza Night*, and they chose that particular night to roost in the big tree out front.

She knew that they were there to watch her bury her pizza crusts, and they planned to fly down and get them when she was finished. I could tell that this absolutely infuriated her, and I watched with interest to see what she would do. She went out in the field to her normal hiding place and dug a little hole. Then she covered it back up with her nose. I saw her look up in the tree when the birds made noises and watched her as she came back towards the house. She had something in her mouth. It was the pizza crust! Ignoring me, she went in under the deck like nothing was going on. After a while, she returned from under the porch from a different location and resumed her pizza crust stare.

I knew about Cowgirl's ongoing feud with the pesky magpies. She had a hatred for those birds. Other times when we were in the field irrigating and a magpie flew over she stopped whatever she was doing and watched them. Her eyes reeked with hatred. It was an ongoing battle with those magpies; she chased them whenever they were around the corrals or the chicken pen. They were not tolerated anywhere near the house while she was on watch.

Magpies had big mouths and were always taunting Cowgirl. They knew how much they bothered and tormented her as they sat on the fence posts, teasing and cackling until she gave chase. Their ongoing feud reminded me of how Satan constantly wants to lie, cheat, and steal from us.

Like Cowgirl, what we value we protect. She protected the ranch, the chickens, the cows; she was on guard at all times. She is a good steward of what she has been placed in charge of. We are to be good stewards of what God has given us as well, our jobs, finances, families and everything that God has blessed us with.

We are called to be wise as serpents and gentle as doves. Satan will take any opportunity to destroy or steal what we value. His mode of attack is to destroy our faith, our relationship with God, our marriages, families, and friendships.

The family is the prized foundation for all of us. It is uniquely designed with a father as the provider and protector alongside the mother who nurtures. Together, they form an intertwined strand when wrapped with the Holy Spirit. This makes for a strong chord that cannot be broken. God designed marriage that way and Satan knows that if he can alter it in any way, it will destroy that uniquely powerful relationship. Look around today. Can you see Satan's hand at work in the world we live?

We have treasures that we store up in Heaven too. When we help someone out, whether they need help for example with food or money or just an ear to talk to, we are storing up treasures in Heaven. Jesus told us to help the widows, orphans, and the poor with clothing, food and water and visit the people in prison. In other words, love on them.

Whether it is time, money or a kind word, they are all valuable to someone. When you store up treasures for Heaven, you do it quietly! The bible says if you tell everyone about the good deeds that you have done you will receive the reward here on earth. If you keep it to yourself then you will be rewarded in Heaven. Take Cowgirl's example; when you are storing up your heavenly treasures, keep it private and don't let the magpies see it!

A Bone to Chew On:

Can you see where Satan is attacking something you value?

What are your treasures? Where are they?

What are some of the ways you protect your treasures?

Are you setting aside treasure for when you get to heaven?

Do you make the effort to help those less fortunate?

Will you make time for someone that just needs an ear to listen to or are you too busy?

Proverbs 6:6 *Go to the ant, thou sluggard; consider her ways, and be wise*

1Peter 5:8 *Be sober, be vigilant; because your adversary the devil, as a roaring lion, walketh about, seeking whom he may devour*

Malachi 2:8*10 *Will a man rob God? Yet ye have robbed me. But ye say, Wherein have we robbed thee? In tithes and offerings. Ye [are] cursed with a curse: for ye have robbed me, [even] this whole nation. **Bring ye all the tithes into the storehouse, that there may be meat in mine house, and prove me now herewith, saith the LORD of hosts, if I will not open you the windows of heaven, and pour you out a blessing,** that [there shall] not [be room] enough [to receive it]."*

Matthew 6:19-21 "Lay not up for yourselves treasures upon earth, where moth and rust doth corrupt, and where thieves break through and steal, But **lay up for yourselves treasures in heaven, where neither moth nor rust doth corrupt, and where thieves do not break through nor steal, For where your treasure is, there will your heart be also**"

Standing in the Gap

The crystal clear reflection of the surrounding green hillsides and giant ponderosa pine trees were shattered as the truck's tires passed through each mud puddle. Merl, my first dog, and I were driving the yellow, three quarter ton Ford pickup back up the long mountain driveway to the ranch house. It was mid-afternoon in early spring, and we were returning from town with groceries. The sun had broken through the heavy clouds which were disappearing quickly after the healthy rain earlier had drenched the ranch. Intermittent wisps of steam or "water dogs" as they are called, drifted carelessly through the trees and up the steep hillsides. "Water dogs" form as a result of the moisture coming into contact with the warming hillsides. I had the window down enjoying the warm sunshine. An occasional splash of muddy water hit my arm from the puddles. The spicy aroma of wild sumac filled the air, intermingling with the scent of pine and the residual morning rain. I heard a wild turkey gobble somewhere up on the hill when I shut the second metal gate midway up the driveway. That sent off a volley of calls from several gobblers up and down the canyon. It was springtime on the breaks of the Clearwater River in Central Idaho.

Merl was little, just a ball of fur really. Julie, my girlfriend at that time and I had picked the little dog out of a litter of nine pups about a week prior. Merl and I were still going through the bonding process. He was an Australian Shepherd/Border Collie cross. His coat was tri-colored, mottled with black, grey and light brown. He had white socks and a white nose that formed a stripe that went between his eyes and over the top of his head spilling into a white collar around his neck. One eye was blue and the other was brown. He had a knob for a tail and when he was happy, his whole butt wiggled. When we were driving in the truck, he sat in my lap with his paws on my arm trying to look out the window. Merl had a little case of separation anxiety, and he whined whenever I got out of the truck to open the gate or get the mail.

As we came up to the hay barn, I noticed that the gate was open. That wasn't right; it was supposed to be shut. We were finished feeding the cows for the winter except for the bull, Brutus, who was in the corral adjacent to the hay shed. Seeing the gate open, my eyes immediately shifted to the corral. Not seeing him there, I looked back to the hay barn and spotted the top of his back behind a round bale. His head was down, and he was gorging on one of the few round bales of alfalfa left. He was a large Simmental bull about four years old and stood a strong six foot at the shoulder. His face was blotched white like someone had taken a large thick paintbrush loaded with white paint and slapped his face with it as he turned away; the rest of him was light reddish brown. He had a tuft of brown hair at the top of his large head that stuck up between his ears which gave him the look of a schoolyard bully. I named him Brutus the first time I saw him and rightly so. His temperament was basically good, but his size was intimidating. Occasionally, he found his way out of the corral and when he did he lavished the whole essence of freedom by bucking around, blowing snot, kicking up his back legs while coming in just close enough to me to make my heart skip a beat. He flaunted his forbidden freedom with an air of arrogance.

As I pulled to a stop, his head immediately came up with both ears pointed towards me completely alert. The tuft of hair between them stuck straight up. He knew he was not supposed to be in the hay shed and he looked like a ten-year-old kid busted with his hand in the cookie jar. It was written all over his face as one of his ears went back, still chewing on a mouthful of sweet alfalfa hay, savoring every last morsel.

I positioned the truck so as to encourage him back towards the corral and discourage him from going down the driveway. When I got out of the truck, his guilt got the better of him, and he started looking for a way out of the situation he had gotten himself into. There was only one easy way out, so as calmly as I could I went through the gate to gently persuade him back around the way he had come in.

The pole barn's front and back were open-ended with the main feeding stanchion on one side and a corrugated tin wall on the opposite side. It was completely surrounded with a tall plank fence around it, about six feet out from the barn. The corrugated tin was on the top and backside to protect the hay from the winter weather. We stacked the round bales against that wall. There was a three foot alleyway between the corrugated back wall and the corral fence which had a section of old feeding stanchions that were no longer used. On the back side of that fence was the bull's corral. In that three-foot alleyway there were little patches of green grass growing.

The bull had nervously relocated near the grass in an attempt to get back into the corral where he knew he was supposed to be. The problem was that he couldn't get back into the corral that way. If I could get him to back down the narrow alleyway which he filled, he could make the turn at the end and would be free. His nostrils were flaring, and I could tell he was nervous. From his perspective, I was blocking his escape route. I didn't want to risk the possibility of him going over the back fence and getting in with the cows. It was too early in the year to turn the bull out and there were yearling heifers intermixed with the cows that we did not want bred by Brutus. I talked to him calmly while I slowly backed him down the alleyway. I was about midway when he reached the end, and his butt hit the back fence. He could have made the corner, but he was feeling cornered and already wrapped like a stick of dynamite. All it would take was a spark for him to explode. He wanted back into the corral even if he had to go through me to do it! When his butt hit that fence and the fence post retorted with a loud crack, he blew. He charged towards me head down at a dead run, fully committed at whatever cost in order to get out of the situation! As fast as he was coming, the only thing I could think to do was jump up on the side of the feeding stanchion, but as I got up to the top there was nothing to hold on to. I started to fall backwards into the alleyway right into his path. I quickly reached out my hand to the corrugated barn wall and let him pass underneath me.

I let out a big sigh of relief as I watched the bull's giant head pass under me. I was about to commend myself for quick thinking when everything unraveled. I hadn't calculated for the hump on his back and when it hit my side, it knocked me loose from the feeding stanchion. I fell on him, and he responded in anger at my rolling across his back and down his side. As I lay on the ground, I felt the cool air brush my head as his large hoof passed me with a mere miss as it connected to the stanchion. The wood siding of the stanchion exploded everywhere with a loud crack sending chips of wood and dirt into my face. With my eyes synched shut, I dared opening only one eye and saw that the nightmare wasn't finished.

When Brutus came to the end of the run, he wheeled around facing me slinging snot towards me. I laid there looking up at him towering over me only twenty feet away.

The whites of his eyes revealed the tension coursing though his body. His sides heaved, and his eyes pierced. He stood firmly planted, his tail whipping. He snorted loudly blowing snot everywhere and lowered his giant head. The once sweet smell of chewed alfalfa on his breath revealed something more sinister. He was no longer the schoolyard bully, he was Satan himself! He looked at me laying there helplessly on the ground like he had every intention of putting an end to this nonsense. I figured this was it.

My dad's words of wisdom echoed in my head, "You have to be extra careful when you are up here by yourself. Don't get yourself in a bad situation that you can't get out of. Use your head!" I realized this was probably what he was talking about!

Then, out of nowhere a little gray fluff of fur jumped between the bull and me, let out a loud awkward bark, shocking both of us. What seemed like a minute was only a fraction of a second – all three of us, frozen in time. It was that second that held life and death in its hand.

Brutus looked down in dismay at the little ball of fur, surveying the new player. His ears twitched nervously and reluctantly decided to finish this at a more opportune time. Letting out a heavy sigh, he turned and trotted out the gate back to the safety of his corral. I grabbed Merl and jumped to my feet brushing the dirt from my pants.

I am not sure if Brutus would have taken me out or not, but I was certainly thankful for that little dog! Merl jumped out of the truck, ran over and stood in the gap between the bull and me. We bonded right there. That began an amazing relationship with my awesome dog.

I saw the unconditional love that Merl gave me every time I looked at him, and to this day I'm still moved by the memories of my little fur ball. He loved me whether life was good or whether Brutus was at the door. Likewise, when God sees that we love Him no matter what trial we are going through it pleases Him so much! He sees the trust that we have in Him. In turn we are given the opportunity to show our love and loyalty to Him for what He has done for us.

Merl stood in the gap at the risk of being trampled. There was little time to think about it, the decision was made in an instant. There will be times in our lives when we might seem like a little ball of fur but if we stand our ground with confidence knowing that Jesus has our back, Brutus will submit and flee.

A Bone to Chew On:

Are you face to face with a bull right now in your life?

Can you see an example of God's love in your dog?

Have you seen the Holy Spirit intercede with you in your life?

How is your relationship with God?

Have you seen God's protective hand where He has stood in the gap for you?

John 3:16-17 *"For **God so loved the world, that he gave his only begotten Son, that whosoever believeth in him should not perish, but have everlasting life**. For God sent not his Son into the world to condemn the world; but **that the world through him might be saved**."*

John 14:26 ***But the Comforter,*** which is ***the Holy Ghost, whom the Father will send in my name, he shall teach you all things,*** *and bring all things to your remembrance, whatsoever I have said unto you.*

Acts 2:21 *And it shall come to pass, that **whosoever shall call on the name of the Lord shall be saved.***

Frank

I had not known Frank long. He believed that I was his nemesis. He was mistaken. Frank's insecurities were deeply rooted from a previous owner who abused him and then discarded him at a shelter for dogs. The abuse and neglect that Frank endured I can only imagine. The life of this wiener dog was tough. Everyone towered over him.

Frank knew what to expect every day. People were constantly stepping on him and kicking him in the ribs. He tried to get out of the way but was longer than most dogs. It took some time to move out of the way! The yelling wasn't too bad because at least they gave him some sort of attention. They at least acknowledged him. After a severe kicking, leaving his ribs broken, he made an extra effort to sit in the corner, out of the way. When people walked by he looked down in submission hoping that they would not kick him again.

Anything was better than when they left him alone outside for days or weeks on end. The countless hours of the sun's penetrating heat beat down on him with little to no shade. He dug down to get the little relief that the cool ground offered. By mid-day the water dish was dry. It was a constant battle fighting the ants for his food. Being chained to a metal stake in the ground, he was not going anywhere. He was alone . . . in solitary confinement. He could see the masters in the house walking around, laughing. All he wanted was to join in with them, and he barked to get their attention. Anything, just a little attention. They came out raising his hopes for some sort of acceptance, only to kick him again for making too much noise or because the neighbor complained. At least it was some attention.

But then after that kick broke his ribs the pain was too much. He made up games instead to keep himself from growing insane. He paced back and forth or ran in circles over and over, wearing the grass down to the bare dirt. He was forced to eat his dinner next to where he went to the bathroom. Yes, the days were brutal, but nothing compared to the nights. They were cold, dark, and the storms came at night. It was miserable being alone in the mud with the driving wind and the relentless rain pounding on his bare back all night. But what really messed his head up were the relentless flashes of lightning. He tried hiding in the hole he had dug but there was little relief. One minute the flashes illuminated everything in sight with blinding light, followed by intense darkness and the colossal "BOOM" of the thunder that rattled everything down to the windows on every house in the neighborhood. It drove him crazy. It made his heart race; if he could have sweat, he would have! So, he panted. There was nowhere to escape! That darn chain! He tried running from it but it wound up on itself and eventually he was wound up so tight against it that the masters had to unwrap him. Then there was no escaping the storm. He had to lay pinned against the stake in the driving rain, panting in shock waiting for the masters to notice him. When they did, they were angry at him! He tried chewing the chain off once, but it broke his teeth. Eventually, his complaining got so bad that they took him away for a ride in the car, in a plastic crate with bars.

Upon arrival at *The Prison,* they took him out and sat him on the counter where they looked him over very carefully, poking and prodding and then stuck him with needles. There were new masters there who talked nicely to him but... there was something... he could smell the fear in the air. Something wasn't right about this place. They carried him to a large building. He was thankful that at least he was out of the weather. This was going to be okay. They opened the door and threw him into a cold, stinking concrete prison along with other angry, tormented and lonely strangers that were growling, barking and gnashing teeth. The confusion was intense.

Every dog reacted differently to this experience. Frank, being a wiener dog, had always looked different than most dogs. He had always endured the name calling because of his long body. His spots were not evenly distributed, and he had to deal with all the comments about that. He tried to ignore it but, honestly, it hurt. He was tired of it all and sat in the corner watching the others in this confusing mess, his eyes bugged out, he shook uncontrollably. "How did I ever get here?" he wondered.

Some of them terrified him. They were much bigger and vicious, striking out at everyone that walked by. He tried his best to avoid them.

Others were quiet, withdrawing deep within themselves, delving into their own lonely thoughts. Deep inside they hurt so badly. Frank understood what they were going through. They were lonely and angry. If someone got too close, they lashed out to make them go away, but it just left them lonelier and angrier. Some curled up in a tight ball and slept, hoping that this was some wild nightmare that had gone terribly wrong. Others yakked all the time - nonstop. There were the ones that stopped eating and others who ate their own food and everyone else's too! Some of the dogs told stories about dogs that had been there a long time. They were taken away by the new masters and never came back.

He heard a black mongrel say to a newcomer, "If no one wants you, after a while they take you away and then they give you a shot with a long sharp needle. It makes you sleep and you never bark or wag your tail again. Then they put you in a plastic bag and throw you in the big, metal, blue box out back. You know that terrible bang you hear? That is the sound of the blue box! Listen for it!" Those images scared Frank. He had heard that bang. It reminded him of the flash of lightening when he was chained to the metal stake. That night he thought of everything the mongrel had said. He was scared and alone. He shook all night into the next day. The corner was his friend.

There were some odd dogs at the place. They were strangely optimistic. Nothing seemed to bother them. He wanted to be like them, but he couldn't shake all this pain and emotional garbage rolled around in his head. No matter what he tried it just wouldn't go away. Frank wondered if the positive dogs were either insane or delusional because they were *always* happy, even in this prison. He was amazed that their tails wagged no matter what happened to them. He also noticed that these dogs never stayed long.

Frank felt discarded like trash in a dark, dirty alley deep in the inner city with giant walls towering around him on all sides. He had been thrown out, unwanted, lost in a prison with little chance of ever escaping. What was he going to do? Jump the walls? He was a wiener dog!

Frank had one pleasant moment that he looked forward to every day. It was to see the sun when it passed overhead casting its warm rays of hope into the depths of the prison.

One day the sun came right inside the building for Frank. A very tall slender lady named Karen stopped by the entrance to Frank's prison. She peered down at him sitting behind the chain link door. Frank looked into

Karen's eyes and saw a warmth that he had longed for all his life but had never felt. She had the kindest eyes and when they locked onto his eyes, there was an instant connection. It was as if she read his whole life in an instant and understood all the abuse and loneliness that he had ever endured.

It scared him when he barked. He had been quiet for so long that he thought that he had forgotten how to bark! Karen laughed at the surprised look on Frank's face! Her laughter was sweet music to him! She was beautiful. He had to do something. He was afraid that she would leave him if she heard or saw all the garbage that he had done in his life. The holes he had dug in the yard, the shoes he had chewed on, the accident on the carpet when they kicked him. And then there were his cracked teeth and the lump on his side from the broken ribs.

Then Frank remembered what the optimistic dogs did. He reached down deep within, and he wagged his tail as hard as he could for Karen. He could tell by the look in her eyes that she noticed. A smile spread across her beautiful face. Karen bent down to Frank and held her hand out. He looked down feeling unworthy but being so drawn to her, slowly lifted his pointy nose and ever so softly licked her hand. She held his little head cradled in her hand and looked in his eyes. There *was* a connection.

Karen understood Frank and what he had been through. There were times in her life where people had treated her the same way. When Karen lifted Frank off the cold concrete and away from the stench of the prison floor, something changed in him. She held him tight, close to her chest as they walked down the cold, dark concrete hallway of the prison and out into the warm sunshine. He knew that she loved him and didn't notice the smell of his past life. That life began to fade the further he got away from the prison. She carried him to the warm room and sat him on the counter. Her reassuring hand never left him as she reached into her purse and paid for his life.

Frank sat in her lap with his head out the window as they drove away. Her hand on his back reassured him, the warmth of the sun shone down on him and the breeze lifted Frank's long ears. Little by little the wind caressed his coat working its way deeper and removing the stench of his past.

We all have the stench of a former life that we pack around. For some of us though it is deep, dark and painful. We do our best to deal with it by ignoring it, tucking it under laughter, hoping it will go away but physical or emotional abuse always leaves a scar. It is not always easy to see, but it is always lingering just under the surface. Anything might trigger an emotional outburst and when it comes, it can be ugly lashing out at the people who are loved the most. Other times it stays hidden deep in our heart causing so much pain that it will never allow us to get close enough to love anyone the way God intended. Inevitably we sabotage relationships so as to not risk hurting again. We look and find every excuse humanly possible to justify why the relationship will not work. Those lies from the enemy may prevent us from experiencing the enjoyment of an incredible journey with someone very special.

Others find themselves in an abusive relationship, whether physical or emotional, and think if they just stay out of the way, they will get enough attention to survive. Inside their head, they do not believe that they deserve a relationship with anyone that would love them the way God intended, so they take what is thrown to them.

Abuse etches into our minds telling lies that we are not worthy of being loved. We're not smart enough, pretty enough, thin enough. These are all lies from Satan to make life so miserable that we cannot function the way God intends us to live. It is Satan's hope that if he can convince us, God won't be able to use us thus debilitating us from service.

When someone lives in that stench for years, it isn't something that can be simply stepped away from. It has been burned into our heads and if allowed, Satan stays there playing that song over and over. Before long the chains in the backyard wind up to the stake, the sun beats down and no water is in the dish leaving a body to dig a hole and crawl into it but knowing that is not even an option.

Be encouraged. God has a plan for everyone and He is continually reaching out to us. All we have to do is reciprocate. Bark, wag a tail, and accept His unconditional love. He will pull each of us out of that hole we have dug. If we are in an abusive relationship, get help and get out of it! God did not intend for us to be in the hands of abusive people.

Dogs are smart when allowed to be. They are very much like us and respond well when they have an assignment. We all thrive when we are loved and have value placed on us. Step into God's love. He loves all of us and we are a highly valued commodity in His eyes.

Sometimes we hole up when we have been abused. One of the quickest ways to get out of that hole is to get our eyes off of ourselves and help someone that may be in dire need of a friend.

Nobody needs to sit in the corner in fear; we can approach our Father anytime. He will lift us up out of the dark prison and into the sun. Let the Holy Spirit cleanse you with His breeze. If you have something going on in your life that you need His help with ask Him. He is your Abba Father and is *always* available to you!

Like Karen was for Frank, Jesus went through abuse too. He knows what you are going through and can relate to where you are. He is willing to go into your dark prison.

All you need to do is call on His name. The price has been paid in full!

A Bone to Chew On:

Are you in an abusive relationship now?

Do you have hidden pain from your past?

Can you see how you hide it?

Has it revealed itself at an inopportune time?

How do you deal with the hidden pain in your life?

Do you think you could help someone else who is going through what you have been through?

John 15:12 *This is My commandment, that you **love one another as I have loved you***

2 Timothy 1:7-8 ***For God has not given us a spirit of fear, but of power and of love and of a sound mind.*** *Therefore do not be ashamed of the testimony of our Lord, nor of me His prisoner,* ***but share with me in the sufferings for the gospel according to the power of God,***

Psalm 23:4 *Yea, though I walk through the valley of the shadow of death,* ***I will fear no evil; For You** are **with me***; *Your rod and Your staff, they comfort me.*

That's Mine

That first blast of cold when Julie and I stepped out of the truck made our nostrils stick together, and a white cloud of moisture escaped from Julie's mouth as she commented how cold it was. The sun was just peeking over the top of the mountain, lighting up the mountainside on the opposite side of the lake. We had accomplished what we set out to do and were the first ones at this prized ice fishing spot. Further down the lake we could see other rigs coming up the road and we knew that we needed to get on the ice to stake our claim where we were going to fish. Merl was completely oblivious to the cold, sticking his nose in the snow, reading every sign left by previous visitors. His satisfaction was completed with a snort and then he moved on to more fascinating information. As we trudged across the ice pulling the sled filled with the auger, tip-ups, bait and tackle, Merl followed from intriguing post to post, logging in all the information and occasionally marking a spot.

By the time we had ten holes drilled, tip-ups baited and in the water, the sun was up. It was still cold but the sunshine made it seem warmer, and Julie relished the warmth permeating from her coffee mug. People were starting to come out onto the lake and pick their fishing spots.

In Idaho and Montana there is an unmentioned rule, or maybe it's not a rule but respect for another fisherman's space. When you come up on a fishing hole and there is someone there, you either politely ask if they mind if you join them or you move on to another spot. No big deal as there are thousands of acres for hunting and fishing. That was the way it was when I was growing up and that is what my dad taught me. Over the years, Idaho and Montana have had many people move there who were not raised in this way and it was always shocking when we ran across those people. We try to ignore them, but it's still unnerving.

Once we had our holes drilled in the ice, we settled into fishing. We noticed three guys headed toward us with their fishing gear. A couple of our tip-up flags went up, so Julie and I each ran to one and worked to bring up the fish. When we were finished bringing them in and re-baiting the hooks, we noticed to our astonishment that the three guys had set up right next to where we were fishing. I mean, they were right next to us. It was like living in one of those subdivisions in the big city!

Julie stated her annoyance to me, and I mumbled to her that they had as much right to be there as we did. However, I was annoyed too, probably more than she was.

I was sitting in one of the chairs intently scanning the tip-ups for another fish to come by and bite when Julie whispered very quietly, "Good dog!" I looked over to see Merl lifting his leg on one of their tip-ups and I laughed nervously. I clicked a call that only Merl knew, and he headed towards me with what looked like a huge grin on his face. I couldn't help but laugh and honestly, as bad as it sounds, I was really very proud of him. I looked over at the three guys who were standing in a tight circle talking to each other and hadn't noticed. It seemed that Merl knew the boundaries even though these guys didn't have a clue. Merl marked where the line was drawn and what was his.

In much the same way, my friend Karen's dog, Frank, also marked his property with a distinct southern flair! Arriving from a long flight from Idaho to Louisiana, Karen walked me up the sidewalk to her front door. I could hear Frank's toenails dancing on the hardwood floor inside. His barks of joy were for Karen, the love of his life. He could be heard even through the solid hardwood door. He anxiously awaited the return of his beloved master longing to spend quality time with her and no one else!

When I stepped into view, Frank's disappointment was immediately apparent. The happiness and joy that he greeted Karen with disappeared in a flash and his whole demeanor changed the second he laid eyes on me. It was like a light switch had been turned off. His head drooped; his tail dropped almost dragging on the ground, barely moving, and he gave me that stink-eyed stare of disdain over his shoulder as he walked down the long, dark, hardwood hallway of his domain. You could almost hear him say, *"You again! I thought I got rid of you last time!"* Watching him disappear around the corner I was amazed how such a short dog managed to look down on me! Little did I know he was forming his plan of retaliation.

As I mentioned earlier, Frank is a wiener dog. Okay, a Dachshund, which I am pretty sure is German for wiener dog. Every time Karen and I would sit on the couch, Frank begged relentlessly until he wore Karen down; then she'd lift him up. Once in her arms and then on her lap, he would work his long nose between the two of us. Sometimes he would climb up on the top of the couch so he could get his face right next to Karen's. He always needed Karen touching him and to be between us.

Every time I visited Karen, Frank found a way to get into the guest room where I'd sleep and plant a land mine. It was about a third the length of a Weiner dog with the same shape and it smelt . . . well, it warned me ahead of time. It usually happened on the second or third day of my visit, so I was pretty sure he saved it up to make an even more dramatic statement. I learned to keep my door shut when I visited.

If you looked in the dictionary for the definition of "jealousy," toward the very bottom it should say, "Frank; or a relation thereof." Dogs want their masters' attention. The dog I have now, Cowgirl, rides in the back seat portion of my extended cab pickup. When someone is riding with me she lays her head on my shoulder and nuzzle my neck as if to say, *"I am still here!"* Or she will stand between the two of us on the center console so I cannot see the person sitting next to me. She is making her presence known, laying claim to her territory in her unique way.

God is like that too. He wants our undivided attention. The Bible says that we serve a jealous God. He wants to be first in your life, and you will see that when you do put Him first everything falls into place. If you have been a Christian for some time, then you most likely experienced this at some time in your life. There will be seasons where you drift away. Life is good and you get busy maybe raising a family or working and before you know it you have stopped praying or might not be reading your Bible as much. God will send things into your life to convict you of that, and if you continue to ignore it, eventually something will happen to get your eyes back on Him. God is patient, but He does want your attention.

A Bone to Chew On:

Is God *Number One* on your list?

Do you make time for Him every day?

Is He the Lord in every area of your life or do you hold some things back?

Has He ever gotten jealous over where your focus is?

How did He let you know?

Deuteronomy 4:23-24 *"Take heed unto yourselves, **lest ye forget the covenant of the LORD your God, which he made with you**, and make you a graven image, or the likeness of any thing, which the LORD thy God hath forbidden thee. **For the LORD thy God is a consuming fire, even a jealous God.**"*

Matthew 14:29-32 *"And he said, Come. And when Peter was come down out of the ship, **he walked on the water, to go to Jesus. But when he saw the wind boisterous, he was afraid; and beginning to sink,** he cried, saying, Lord, save me. And immediately Jesus stretched forth his hand, and caught him, and said unto him, O thou of little faith, wherefore didst thou doubt? And when they were come into the ship, the wind ceased."*

Stop, Sit and Stay...
Focused

The day came to turn Merl out on the cows. He had to start earning his keep around the ranch. It was the spring of 1987 and a perfectly beautiful day. I needed to move the cows from one pasture to the other and thought this might be a good time to turn him loose to give him a little experience. The cows all knew what they were supposed to do so this should not have been a problem whatsoever. Merl and I were riding the four-wheeler behind the herd, and Merl was excited, anxious to help out with this new exciting assignment.

I figured that he was ready when there were a couple of yearlings that had an idea of going in a completely different direction. I sent Merl off after them, and he did great! He headed them off and got them to run back towards the herd with no problem. I was pleased with him, but then to my astonishment, he went right to the front of the herd and everything fell apart. He confronted the lead cows and got right in their faces causing them to split off going in every direction! I was hollering at him to stop but he was not listening. I'm sure in his mind, he thought he was the greatest herdsman that had come to the ranch, and I was cheering him on! *How awesome am I? My master should be downright lucky to have my help!* When he finally realized that I was yelling at him and not at the cows it was too late. They were so spread out and deep in the brush that it took another half a day to get them out!

For the next few weeks we tried moving cows on a smaller scale multiple times with basically the same result. Merl could not get this figured out. He was great at turning a stray cow, but when it came to the main herd, he would get right in the front and break up the entire herd. This infuriated my dad and eventually I kept Merl on the back of the four-wheeler barking and using him for strays. I would send him off on little assignments and then call him back to the four-wheeler. It took some time, but with persistence he finally got herding cows figured out and became invaluable. Once we had all the cows in the corral, he would assume his position on the four-wheeler and sit there all day long waiting for further directions. His eyes were always focused on me. I would look up to make sure he wasn't getting into trouble, and he would be sitting on the four-wheeler or close by; but he always had one eye on me and what I was doing. If I called him he was instantly ready to go to work.

On one occasion a few years later, I went into town to get some things for work. It took a little bit of time to get everything I needed. When I came out of the store and was walking across the parking lot, a guy hollered for me. I went over to his truck. He was an older gentleman and he asked me what kind of dog Merl was. I told him that he was an Australian Shepherd. He said that he had never seen a dog so focused on his master before.

I said, "Really? How do you mean?"

"I have been watching your dog since you left. He watched you go into the store and his eyes never left the door after you went inside!" He said, "I tried everything to get his attention. I honked, hollered and whistled at him, and he would not even glance at me. I even threw a piece of my sandwich in the back of the truck but his eyes never left the entrance. That is an amazing dog!"

"Good thing you didn't have a cat or a squirrel!" I thought to myself.

When Jesus was walking on the water, He called Peter to walk to Him and when Peter started getting his eyes off of Jesus and focused on the waves around him he started to sink. It is so easy for us to lose focus with the distractions going on around us. The Bible says that if we keep our eyes focused on Him, He will direct our paths. However, this is not a one-sided agreement. We need to trust that He will direct our paths even when God is silent. When we take our eyes off Him and what He is doing, we tend to sink too. Do you ever wonder why you are going through so many quiet times with the Lord? I think He is trying to teach us to stop, sit, and stay... focused. Maybe it's like Merl herding cows; he couldn't grasp what I needed him to do the first time so I gave him smaller assignments that he could achieve. He had to start small and work up to bigger tasks once he understood. Some tasks are more difficult for us to grasp than others. Sitting tight when we don't hear from our Master tends to make our eyes wander off in another direction, and heaven forbid if a squirrel or a cat walks by!

One day last year I was driving home from work, and as I drove up to the ranch, I could see one of the yearling heifers had gone through the fence and was eating from the hay stack. This knot-head heifer was forming a bad habit of getting out and causing trouble. The week before, I came home to find that she had gotten out and was chewing on the seat of the four-wheeler; which happened to be sitting in the garage! She was getting to be a pain in the butt and her prophetic future was quickly involving an auction or someone's dinner plate. She was wearing on my patience! Most of the time the cows were good; they knew when they got out that it was not where they were supposed to be. All I needed to do was holler and they would run back into the pasture, bucking like mischievous kids. This yearling was flat out *rebellious*!

When I reached the house, I grabbed a whip and tried to push her around back through the gate next to the haystack. Each time she would bypass the gate and run around the hay stack staying just ahead of me and out of sight. She would hear me coming, grab a mouthful of hay, wait for me to catch up and look back taunting me. Cowgirl walked with me and after circling the haystack a couple of times, I signaled Cowgirl with hand commands to sit and stay just beyond the gate while I pushed the heifer around the haystack. Cowgirl could not see me when I went around the haystack. The heifer was having a lot of fun leading the ole' farmer-guy in circles and almost tripped over herself when she went around the corner and saw Cowgirl blocking her path!

All of the cows had respect for Cowgirl. She had let them know she was in charge. That was her job description and she was *all* business. When that heifer saw Cowgirl crouched low and focused on her with an intense stare, the game stopped immediately! The heifer decided right then and there that she didn't want to play anymore and couldn't wait to get back in the pasture.

Sometimes God just tells us to wait. *Ugh*…. I know! Waiting is good though. It produces patience and builds trust. It also makes us more apt to get things done at the appropriate time, when it needs to be done, instead of running around in circles and having to go back and round everything up again.

I think about how many times He has told me to stop, sit and stay. The unspoken *focused* part was the hardest. Like Merl, patience has not always been easy for me; maybe not for you either. I figured that I knew what God was doing and before long, I was out ahead and had cows going every direction too.

My intentions were always big, and I knew that He was going to be so proud of me helping Him to achieve what needed to be done faster than He had originally planned. Stop, sit and stay was not in my vocabulary. Mine was more like "Get off your butt and get it done, *Right now*! We're burning daylight!"

If you are anything like me, God is still proud of us considering the mess we tend to make. I imagine He probably appreciates our work ethic and our desire to work so hard for Him. That being said, it is good that He loves us so much and has patience for those He loves. He always has a way of working things out, but I think He gets it done much faster and more efficiently when we do it His way.

My friend, Karen said it this way, "we can all see down the road for a bit and think it is safe to cross, but we cannot see down the road and around the corner like God can."

The Bible is full of examples where people got out ahead of Him. Abraham and Sara are a perfect example. In Genesis 15:5-17:22, God told Abraham that he would have decedents that would outnumber the stars in the skies. As they aged, Abraham and Sara decided that they needed to help God out a little by using Sara's bond servant. However that wasn't exactly what God had in mind.

There is a time for everything and so often when God is having us sit and wait, He is doing something behind the scenes out of our view. Much of the time He is working on us, changing us, conforming us, building our patience and teaching us to trust in Him. Sometimes though He is lining things up for something or someone else and it has nothing to do with us. You can be sure of one thing; His timing is perfect and when He tells us to wait, He hasn't forgotten about you. When you are in the waiting mode, it is just best to stay focused! Keep one eye open and be ready to move because when He does call you, you better be ready because it's about to get exciting!

I heard someone once ask, "Why does it take so long for God to do something so fast?"

A Bone to Chew On:

Do you feel that you have been ahead of God?

Has he ever told you to stop and wait?

How did you handle waiting?

Do you trust God when you can't see what He is up to?

Do you know what your assignment is?

Will you be ready when He calls you into action?

Psalm 37:3-7 *Trust in the LORD, and do good; [so] shalt thou dwell in the land, and verily thou shalt be fed.* **Delight thyself also in the LORD; and he shall give thee the desires of thine heart.** *Commit thy way unto the LORD; trust also in him; and he shall bring [it] to pass. And he shall bring forth thy righteousness as the light, and thy judgment as the noonday.* **Rest in the LORD, and wait patiently for him: fret not thyself** *because of him who prospereth in his way, because of the man who bringeth wicked devices to pass*

James 5:7-8 *Be patient therefore, brethren, unto the coming of the Lord. Behold,* **the husbandman waiteth for the precious fruit of the earth, and hath long patience for it, until he receive the early and latter rain.** *Be ye also patient; establish your hearts: for the coming of the Lord draweth nigh.*

Proverbs 3:5-8 **Trust in the LORD with all thine heart; and lean not unto thine own understanding. In all thy ways acknowledge him, and he shall direct thy paths.** *Be not wise in thine own eyes: fear the LORD, and depart from evil. It shall be health to thy navel, and marrow to thy bones.*

Temptation

My dogs have always gone everywhere with me. Consequently, it was imperative that they obey due to my high-risk occupations. Everywhere I went had the potential to be life threatening for them, myself or others. If they did not listen and obey, then someone could get hurt, or worse. Obedience was mandatory. When moving cows, they needed to be able to follow instructions with verbal commands as well as hand signals. Both dogs were smart and fairly easy to train if I was consistent with the training. They were always eager to learn and had a desire to please but even that sometimes created a problem. They had to learn to stop when I said stop.

More loyal dogs could not be found, anywhere. That being said, they both put obedience to the test when it came to cats or squirrels. We all have our limits! I could leave a steaming hot hamburger dripping with all the trimmings, topped with cheese and bacon on the dash of the truck, unwrapped. I could leave either one of the dogs in the cab, walk in to a bass fishing store, take my time buying a new fishing rod, having line put on the reel, and buy all the fishing gear for a weekend of phenomenal bass fishing. When I returned to the truck not a morsel of hamburger would be touched, and they would be curled up in the seat. But if a cat or a squirrel walked by the truck, they would be a convulsing mess, wide-eyed, panting and quivering uncontrollably, begging for permission to pursue that despicable excuse of an animal! I am absolutely positive that is what they fantasize about as they lay in front of the woodstove on cold winter nights.

Each one had their personalities and limitations unique to them. When Merl was just a pup, about eight months old, I ran into town to pick up some lumber for a job. A trip into town was a treat for Merl. He knew where every dog lived on the way to town, and although he was normally quiet in the back of the truck, he would announce his approach when we neared a place that had a dog in hopes that he might catch a glimpse as we passed by. He was a socialite! Merl always had his eyes peeled on the road ahead for the ultimate enemy . . . cats and squirrels. He lost any sense of perspective when he saw one cross the road ahead of us. He went on full alert. His focus was virtually unbreakable. I would say his name, and the only way I knew that he could hear me was that his ears would relax for a split second, but his eyes never departed from the suspect. His fascination for them caused him to lose focus completely on every other level even to the point of his own demise. Cats and squirrels were the cause of pure, blind, uncontrollable, and lustful temptation.

After parking in the lumberyard parking lot, I told him to stay in the truck. Until that point he had always stayed, but I feared that one day he would put it to the test as we all do at one time or another. I was standing at the counter waiting in line for my turn to be waited on, and glanced out at Merl sitting in the back of the yellow three-quarter ton Ford. His ears were up and he was intently focused on something. I followed his line of sight across the street to a couple of squirrels innocently frolicking in a grassy park. I had just whispered in my head, *"Don't do it, buddy!"* when, in an instant, he was out of the truck and hell-bent-for-election across the road, chasing the squirrels up a tree! He was so focused on the squirrels that he had not paid attention before crossing the road. From my location, I couldn't yell at him to stop. My anxious heart dropped as I watched the scene unfold in a matter of seconds. Fortunately, there were no cars coming. I left my position in line and went across the road where we had a little conversation. It was made known to him that his decision was not a wise one.

Merl had absolutely no will power when it came to squirrels. One day at the ranch in Peck, Idaho a pine squirrel made the grave mistake of crossing the ranch on its quest to conquer new lands. I was changing the oil in the tractor and noticed that Merl was intently staring into a giant ponderosa pine tree. After finishing, I walked over to see what had captured his attention. High up on a limb sat a little pine squirrel. He was taunting Merl by letting out a series of tormenting chatters. Merl sat patiently waiting. I looked around and there were no other trees close by so knew that this poor little critter was going to have to come down out of the tree to get away. Feeling bad for the little guy I told Merl to back off, come over to the porch and lay down. He obeyed and I went into the house to make lunch. I quickly forgot about the treed squirrel and got distracted doing other things in the house. Dinner time came and I noticed that Merl was not on the porch. I looked outside, and he was sitting at the base of the tree looking up at the little squirrel. Again, I called him back to the porch and scolded him more sternly. He dropped his head and avoided looking back at the squirrel. At bedtime, I went out to check on things, and once again Merl was not on the porch. I looked out under that tree, and there he was staring at the squirrel, even in the dark! I knew the squirrel was not going to leave in the middle of the night so figured that I would take care of this once and for all in the morning.

I woke early to do chores. When I walked outside guilt poured out of Merl who was sitting under the tree. He had worn a path around the tree from circling. When our eyes met; he hung his head in total repentant shame. He knew he had done what he was not supposed to do. I gave him the look like my dad gave me when I was a kid. That look could just about turn me inside out! It was a look that could be seen for a hundred yards through a crowd of hundreds of people in the middle of the state fair but carried implications that were crystal clear. That look could stop any activity immediately, and it affected everyone you were associated with as well. I knew the look well and understood its powerful impact.

Merl responded immediately. He avoided eye contact. His ears relaxed and his head dropped. If he had a tail he would have tucked it between his legs. The guilt was so intense that he looked like a beaten dog. He retreated to the porch and laid down without me saying a word. It took all he had to look up at me. He was ashamed! I called him to me. Reluctantly he came over with his head down. When he reached my feet, he sat and looked up at me with his eyes half open. He knew he was guilty and had to take whatever punishment was due. Lowering my head down to within inches of his nose I said, "What did I tell you?" His eyes blinked nervously and he burped. (Merl burped whenever he was nervous.) I ordered him to the truck because I knew the only way to settle this encounter was to remove him from the temptation. I told him to *"load up"*. He was in the truck within seconds.

Walking over to the tree I told the squirrel. *"This is your chance buddy, you best take it!"* When we got back from town the squirrel was gone.

There is nothing worse than the stern look from a parent or guardian. Whether we want to admit it or not, we all know when we have crossed the line. The Bible says that we all have been given a good measure of right and wrong. Like Merl, we can always find a way to justify succumbing to the temptation, and ignore the warnings that our Father gives us. Sooner or later we will pay for our thrills!

A Bone to Chew On:

I bet you have a pretty good idea of some of your own temptations.

Do you think Satan knows what they are?

Do you take the precautions to avoid the weak areas where you're tempted?

Has God ever had to take something from your life to get your attention?

Can you see when you resist the devil your life goes smoother?

Mathew 6:13 **And lead us not into temptation, but deliver us from evil:** *For thine is the kingdom, and the power, and the glory, for ever. Amen.*

Luke 22:40 *And when he was at the place, he said unto them,* **Pray that ye enter not into temptation**

James 4:7 *Submit yourselves therefore to God.* **Resist the devil, and he will flee from you**

Unqualified

Instinctively, I let off the gas as my friend Leonard
grabbed for the dash. A huge gust of wind rocked the
truck and camper violently. It felt like we were going to
be blown off the road. We were driving on Highway 2
across the Hi-Line headed towards Sydney, Montana.
This was going to be one of those epic hunting trips that
we dreamed about for months! We were going to be
hunting mule and whitetail deer as well as antelope, but
the highlight of the trip was pheasant hunting on a
private ranch in Northeastern Montana.

Leonard had just told me, again, how amazing his bird
dog was and how well it was trained. He had paid eight
hundred dollars for this dog. The bloodline of this
animal rivaled the Queen of England. It was registered
from one of the most revered German Shorthair
Pointers that apparently had ever stepped foot on the
face of the earth. To hear him talk, the Wise Men
owned one of its ancestors, and it surely was
instrumental in locating the Christ Child! It had been
trained by an equally proficient trainer exclusive to
German Shorthairs. I had the honor of driving this
amazing dog which was in a kennel in the back of the
truck.

I looked over at Merl, who was riding in the front seat between the two of us. He was staring intently at the road, I assumed watching for one of those despicable cats or some other varmint that might cross. This was probably the tenth time that Leonard had told me about his dog. He had invited me on this hunting trip to Northeastern Montana a couple months ago. I agreed to go with him but informed him that I would be taking Merl, my bird dog. He had laughed hysterically. "Why would you bring that cow dog bird hunting?"

I told him that Merl was a good bird dog; he just didn't point like one. He wiggled his butt when he was "birdy" and I just needed to pay attention.

He reluctantly agreed to the condition but never missed an opportunity to comment on Merl's inability to hunt birds.

We hunted antelope the first morning and were both successful. Back at the ranch, we skinned and hung them in the barn to cool. After lunch, we decided to do a little pheasant hunting before the whitetail hunt started that evening. Jim, the ranch foreman, showed us which fields we could hunt and where to park our rig. Anticipation for this part of the hunt had been building for me. This was going to be one of those once in a lifetime pheasant hunting experiences.

Merl sat next to my feet sensing my eagerness. It was time to see what an eight-hundred-dollar birddog was like, and I had looked forward to watching Leonard's dog in action. I planned to keep Merl well out of the way so as to not interfere with this art form in action. The last thing I wanted to hear all the way home was how Merl messed up the whole hunting trip by getting in the way.

As he was loading shotgun shells, Leonard looked like he had stepped right out of a hunting magazine advertisement dressed in top of the line hunting pants equipped with brush guard protection, a freshly pressed red hunting shirt, a brand new bright orange hunting cap and Cabela's finest hunting vest. I was envious of his brand-new hunting boots which were equipped with the latest Thinsulate material. His shotgun was a Beretta 12 gauge over and under. When he took it out of the case, it looked like it had never had a shell in it.

Next to Leonard, I felt like a hick dressed in old faded Levis with scarred leather boots that I had worn fighting fires. I still had on the tan, long sleeved shirt I had worn earlier that morning and noticed the blood stains on the sleeves from gutting out the antelope. My old hunting vest had sentimental value; my dad had passed it down to me when I was barely big enough to wear it. It was so old that it didn't have elastic to hold the 16 gauge shells. He had also passed down the worn Model 97 Winchester pump action I was loading. It was old enough to retire and hang on the wall, but it shot where I aimed it.

We stood next to the kennel in great anticipation as Leonard bent over to open the door. I am not sure exactly what I expected but was pretty sure it wasn't what happened. As soon as there was a slight resemblance of daylight in the door, the dog burst out, all but knocking Leonard over. Leonard yelled at the top of his lungs and blew his dog whistle for the dog to stop, but he was gone. I could tell where he was by the pheasants that burst from the heavy cover as he worked across the field.

I learned new applications to words that day from Leonard, and he unloaded his gun a couple of times trying to get the dog's attention. It didn't work. Merl and I stood there not really knowing what to do. I wanted to go hunting, but Leonard's red face made me wonder if that was still on the agenda. He grumbled and walked in the direction that the dog ran madder than a hornet. A giant rooster took a gamble and took off right next to him cackling like the world was coming to an end. Leonard raised up to shoot and nothing happened. He was out of shells! I tried not to laugh watching him scramble to load his gun. He walked back and I couldn't contain myself or my laughter, which made him even more irate! I let him stomp his feet for a bit and said, "Well, are you ready to go hunting?"

He looked at me with a very unfriendly stare and said, "We don't have a dog!"

"Yeah, we do!" I said, looking at Merl.

He mumbled, "Whatever," as he pulled his bright orange hunting cap snugly on his head and started walking towards the field. I figured Leonard needed to walk a little anyway to work things out. It would help to get his mind off his frustration. I was pretty sure his dog was going to be gone awhile anyway; it had been cooped up in the kennel for a long time.

I told Merl to, "Get the birds!" glanced over at Leonard and tried not to smile. Leonard ignored me.

Merl went out into the field, turned, and looked back at me. I said, "Yup, go get 'em!" He turned and stood up on his hind legs to look over the tall cover. He was looking for cows or hopefully, in his mind anyway, a cat. Seeing none, he returned to all fours and then bounced up and down out into the field like a coyote hunting mice. On one of his return bounds, he landed on a rooster pheasant that had been sitting tight. It erupted with a loud cackle as it went airborne between us. Leonard pulled up and fired twice not phasing the bird. The pheasant was getting pretty far out there when I pulled the trigger, and it tumbled to the ground, leaving feathers drifting in the breeze. We jumped several other birds with the same result. Leonard was having one of those days where he could not hit a thing. I felt bad for him. We came to the end of the field and circled around to head back to the truck when he stepped on a rooster that was sitting tight. He turned and fired at the erupting bird rolling it in a cloud of feathers.

99

"Nice shot!" I said walking over to where Merl was standing with a feather on his nose.

He had found where the bird had landed and nuzzled it but wouldn't pick it up. I picked up the bird and with a smile handed the bird to Leonard, who had walked over to where we were. He exclaimed how pleased he was with that new shotgun that he had bought and how he had finally got it dialed in. I agreed with him and mentioned how well Merl located that bird. He rolled his eyes and walked back to his position to hunt the field effectively.

Once Merl figured out what we were hunting, his focus adapted. After a couple of hours, we both had our limit of birds. Merl had done exceptionally well at pointing the birds and locating the downed birds in the heavy cover. We both commented how it was one of the finest pheasant hunting experiences we ever had.

Leonard was relieved to see that his dog was lying next to the truck when we got back. He was covered in mud, completely exhausted with his tongue hanging out, but I had to do a double take when I noticed that it looked like his dog had grown a beard. The closer we got it became apparent that his eight-hundred-dollar dog had found himself a porcupine. I had never seen a dog with so many porcupine quills in its mouth.

We put the dog in the kennel and drove back to the ranch where Jim called the vet that he used for his cattle business. It was late afternoon when we dropped his dog off in town at the Veterinarian's office.

Merl and I sat in the truck when we went back to town to pick up his dog the next day. Leonard's face was flushed with embarrassment when he came out of the Veterinarian's Office. They had to put the dog to sleep to get all the quills out, and he was still a little loopy. I helped Leonard get the dog back into the plastic kennel. Leonard was quiet on the way back to the ranch. I didn't ask and he didn't say how much the bill was, but I figured that he now had a dog well worth over a thousand dollars! Funny thing was, he never said a thing about his dog all the way home.

Sometimes we can get a preconceived idea about how things are supposed to go for us in our life. But God designed you uniquely different than anyone else. The Bible says that He knew you before you were even formed in the womb! He has a plan for you and your life! He knows your potential even though you cannot see it yourself! When I think of that, I think of Gideon. Gideon was hiding in the wine press, threshing wheat, afraid that his enemies, the Midianites, who were going to kill him. An angel came to him and said, "The Lord is with you, you mighty man of valor!" Read that again, Gideon was in the *winepress threshing wheat*. You don't thresh wheat in a winepress; you thresh wheat in a mill. A mill is in the open where the wind can blow the chaff away! Gideon was terrified that he would be killed by the Midianites so he hid in a dark secluded wine press while threshing wheat. God had a plan for Gideon and wanted to use him because Gideon was unqualified. But God knew Gideon's heart; that he would be willing to be used by God even against insurmountable odds.

I encourage you to read the story about Gideon. (It begins in Judges 6:11) It is amazing to see how God used him, even reducing his army to the point of being grossly outnumbered for a battle. Gideon, with God's backing, overcame them against impossible odds. The Lord knew the potential of Gideon even when Gideon had no clue! You would be shocked to see how God sees you. He sees us as the finished product and not the way we are right now. We cannot even remotely grasp the potential that God has given us in Christ. He has already paid the cost for our sins and He is waiting for us to stop by and pick up the receipt and use the power that He has given us through the Holy Spirit! What are you waiting for?

Like Merl and bird hunting, the Lord likes to use unqualified people to do what He needs to get done. By using these people, He shows us and others that He is, in fact, the one doing it through us and it is not just us who are doing it. Consider what God has asked you to do. Does your lack of qualifications stop you? Don't jump ship, obey God and trust in His ability not your eight-hundred-dollar bird dog to get the job done.

A Bone to Chew On:

How often do things turn out the way you plan them?

Do you sometimes feel like you're a cow dog out to do a bird dog's job?

Do you keep an eye out for what the Lord is doing around you?

Are you ready to join in and help Him with what He is doing no matter how unqualified you are?

1 Corinthians 1:27 *"But God hath chosen the foolish things of the world to confound the wise; and God*

1 Corinthians 1:26-27 *For ye see your calling, brethren, how that not many wise men after the flesh, not many mighty, not many noble,* are called:

But God hath chosen the foolish things of the world to confound the wise; and God hath chosen the weak things of the world to confound the things which are mighty;

Sometimes You Fall Out of the Truck

An accident in mid-life required that I make dramatic changes in direction. It was a crisis too, but I didn't feel the urge to buy a hot red car with a sunroof. Out of necessity I moved into town and went back to school. The college I attended was in Lewiston, Idaho. My folks lived by the river, and I lived up in the part of town they called "The Orchards." It was nice to stop in and visit with them, and occasionally they spoiled me with lunch or dinner.

One afternoon I had a meeting scheduled downtown. I was running late, and the temperatures were soaring so I planned to drop Merl off at home before going to the meeting so he wouldn't be waiting in a hot truck. When we lived in Montana, and it got too hot he would jump out of the back of the truck and sit in the shade underneath. He was a smart dog, but the temperatures got much warmer in Lewiston, and it had been reaching into the upper 90's to over 100 degrees. It was too hot for a dog to be sitting under a rig.

My truck was a farm truck and had no tailgate. Merl had a bad habit of standing at the edge of the back of the truck when it came to a stop. I worried about him falling out of the truck when I took off from a stop sign, and I was constantly on him to get closer to the cab. Because he liked to push the edge, I kept a close eye on him, especially when I took off from a stop sign. This particular day, I was in a hurry to go to the meeting and went through stop signs at a rolling stop. I was quite shocked when I got back up to the house and Merl was not in the truck. Actually, I freaked out! *Surely, I didn't leave him at my folks' place, did I?* I called and my folks said that he wasn't there. I drove up and down that stretch of highway and he was nowhere to be found. He had just disappeared! I wanted to throw up! I half-heartedly went to the meeting and came back up that stretch of highway. Still nothing.

When I got back up to the house, I sat down on the couch staring blankly outside. The house was quiet and empty. Merl didn't make a lot of noise but just his presence brightened up the place, loudly. Tears rolled down my cheek as I wondered where he was. Was he alive, or was he lying in the ditch somewhere? If he was alive, what was going through his mind. He probably thought I had abandoned him. I imagined him hitting the pavement hard and rolling down the hot, hard asphalt, tumbling to a stop at the side of the road with gravel embedded in his hide. Maybe some hair was missing from the initial contact. He probably didn't even yelp because he was so caught off guard. I could see him getting to his feet in shock, shaking the dust from his coat, almost falling over still dizzy. Could he have tried to catch up to the truck as it disappeared up the road and out of sight? His heart would have sunk when he could no longer hear the rumble of the exhaust up the canyon. I imagined how he probably thought that I had noticed his falling out of the truck and I'd return for him in minutes. I had never left him stranded before. Would he think that I was not coming back for him? Would he be able to get the coordinates straight in his head to find his way back to the house after such a tumble? I pictured him with his tongue hanging out in the scorching, hot sun limping his way back up the hill on the side of the road. Cars honking at him, he would turn to catch a glimpse of me coming back for him, his hope gradually fading as each one passed him by. Would he give up all together after one of them swerved at him? It was a cruel world, anything could have happened.

Several hours passed since the meeting, and I wondered if he thought that I had given up on him and left him to survive on his own; after all, he had been warned multiple times. Was he punishing himself for pushing the edge that last time? That thought probably made his head hang down a little more. I imagined him thinking, "If I ever get back in that truck I will never stand on the edge again! I promise!"

The thoughts going through my mind upset me. I paced back and forth. I had raised him to stay put when I left him somewhere and hoped that he would do as I taught him. There were so many variables that could have happened to send him in another direction. Did someone stop and pick him up and take him away? I had to go look again.

It was about 5:00 p.m. and I decided to retrace my steps slowly back down to my folks' place. My heart was broken. I had lost my dog, my buddy, my friend. I felt like my heart had been ripped in half. I came up to a stop sign, looked both directions before taking off when I suddenly noticed Merl sitting on the front step of the house on a corner. He was just sitting there on guard, watching over the place.

At first, I was shocked to see him and had to blink my eyes several times to make sure that it was really him! There was no mistaking, it was him. The joy and love for my dog poured through my heart in that instant, it was indescribable. I sat for a second looking at him. I was proud of him waiting there. He learned well what I taught him. His ears were forward and he was focused. So focused that I wondered if there was a squirrel or a cat close by!

I revved up the motor in the truck, and he whipped his head around looking in my direction.

I said, "Hey, what are you doing over there?" His ears relaxed, recognized my voice as pure joy and happiness flooded his being. He ran for the truck, butt wiggling at a dead run. He was about to cross the road and get in the truck when I said, "Whoa!" He stopped and sat down immediately ears back and somewhat shocked looking around. I looked in both mirrors and, seeing no traffic, opened my door and said, "Okay." He jumped over my lap and into the front seat where he sat and barked at me for the next couple of minutes, telling me just how bad it was being left there, and for me never to leave him like that again! I laughed, agreeing wholeheartedly, thankful that he was smart enough to sit tight and stay focused until I got back to get him.

It is like that for us too. Sooner or later whether it is by accident or self-inflicted we fall out of the truck. God gives us *free will*, and sometimes in our infinite wisdom we choose to exercise *free will* in a way that isn't wise. I am sure you have heard the scripture about pride coming before the fall. There are times when we like to ride close to the edge of the tailgate, where the wind blows our hair a little more. It is exciting, at first, then we get prideful and push our limits, riding the edge! We play around with the temptation even when God tells us to get in the truck where it is safer! When we are not paying attention, sin comes along, knocks us off balance and we fall out of the truck.

We are fortunate that God loves us so much that when we fall it breaks His heart too. He knows it is our *free will* when we fall but still He searches for us, wherever we are. He hopes we will return to Him through our own *free will*. God makes Himself available to us but we need to respond. That is our gift of *free will*, and we exercise it in many relationships.

Family love is great and it is a special kind of love, but it is different than a *free will* kind of love. When you give the gift of yourself and your love to someone on your own *free will* it is a very special gift, simply because it is a choice. No one can control our love but us. That is why it hurts when someone takes their love away from us. Think of your best friend. They want to be with you because they love you; they like your company; they understand you and your quirkiness. There will be times when you won't agree with each other or one of you might do something that hurts the other, but reconciliation occurs because they love and value the relationship. It is the same way with marriage. It is an honorable and a highly treasured relationship based on honesty and trust, but it is a choice you make every day to honor that relationship. God wants that same relationship with us.

When we fall out of the truck, God drops everything and comes looking for us because He loves us dearly. Think about that... the relationship that God, the Creator of the Universe, has with you is precious to Him. He wants the same love in return! Our love is a highly valued and sought-after gift that cannot be expressed any other way than through the choice of *free will!*

God is amazing; He will search for you no matter where you are, no matter what you have done, and He will meet you anytime.

No matter how good you think we are, there will always be the possibility that sometime in our life we could fall out of the truck. It could come in the way of flirting with temptation, or it might sneak up on us completely unaware over the years. We might become complacent and one day wake up and realize, I haven't heard from God in a long time!

When God's people become lost He is faithful to search them out and bring them back. He proved that with His son, Jesus. In the beginning when Adam and Eve were walking with Him in the Garden they had a perfect relationship with God, there was no sin. Satan tempted them which eventually led to the disobedience or sin which ultimately changed the relationship that they had with God. That is what sin does. It separates us from God. When Adam and Eve sinned, it caused mankind to fall out of the truck so to speak. But they fell out of the truck by their own *free will*. So, think about it, God created us; what is the point of creating something and making it mandatory that they love you? That's not love. God wants pure, true love. God had to do something to restore that relationship with us that sin separated so He sent His only Son to pay for that sin to restore that relationship. He gives us the choice to love Him back if we chose to do that with our *free will*. That decision is to accept His free gift of Jesus dying for payment for our sins. Because man left through free will, He expects us to return to Him by *free will*. That is true love. Our reward for following Him with our *free will* is eternal life. He will search you out and make Himself available to you but you need to meet Him and get back in the truck! Jesus is saying, *"What are you doing over there?"*

A Bone to Chew On:

Has God ever told you to stop or turn away from something?

Did you stop or did you linger and flirt with the temptation?

How long was it before you fell out of the truck?

Have you ever realized that you had drifted away from God?

Can you remember when God came looking for you?

Have you experienced the grace of God?

Luke 15:10 *"Likewise, I say unto you, **there is joy in the presence of the angels of God over one sinner that repenteth"***
(Read about the Prodigal Son in Luke 15:10 -32.)

James 1:12 ***Blessed is the man that endureth temptation: for when he is tried, he shall receive the crown of life***, which the Lord hath promised to them that love him.

Ephesians 2:8 *"**For by grace are ye saved through faith; and that not of yourselves: it is the gift of God, Not of works, lest any man should boast.***"*

Unconditional Love

There's a joke I heard a while back. It goes something like this: If you want to know who truly loves you, put your spouse and your dog in the trunk of your car for an hour and then see which one is the happiest to see you when you open it!

Okay, that's a little extreme, but it's funny because we all know the personality of a dog and their unconditional love, and we also know how we would feel if we were locked in a trunk for an hour.

I know it is hard to believe, but God loves us more than our dog loves us! His love for us is even greater than a *dog's love*. It is perfect and complete. He loves us to the point that sometimes He allows us to go through tough times to transform us into a more complete person who resembles Him. He knows us better than we know ourselves, and He knows how to get our attention when we stray. He knows exactly what we need to go through to bring us back around. He also knows how we will grow as we go through those tough times. His love is absolute, and although it is not pleasant going through difficult seasons, it's comforting to know that He is right there with us.

You have probably gone through times where you have felt so completely alone, or maybe you're going through that right now. Maybe a divorce, a loved one cheated, or someone you dearly loved passed. There is a void in your heart for that person who has worked their way into your life and now they are gone whether they hurt you intentionally or unintentionally. Dogs seem to know when we are hurting. They are sensitive and tuned in to what we are going through.

I once lost someone I dearly loved. I didn't really lose her through death she simply walked away with someone else. The pain was intense. It would have actually been easier if she would have died. The pain was real to the point of being physically debilitating. It was numbing to the bone. My muscles had no strength; they were empty, lifeless. I felt immobilized. I knew that I needed to shake it but no matter how hard I tried I couldn't. Friends would tell me that I needed to laugh and move on. It was as though she had ripped my beating heart out of my chest and threw it on the highway in front of me while I watched helplessly from the side of the road as cars drove over and over the top of it.

Perhaps you have had a similar experience. No matter what you did you could not remove yourself from that pain. From past experience, you know that only the slow methodical essence of time will provide relief. You cry out to God on your knees, and with all your heart you plead with Him to *please* take the pain away, but there's no response. You feel so alone. It is hard to laugh or feel any emotion. There is nothing but emptiness. If you know God, you know He is with you, but no matter how much you cry out to Him, He is silent. In times like this, you want to hear an audible voice or a hand on your shoulder, but there is nothing.

I remember being on my knees with tears running down my face uncontrollably while I cried out to God for healing. I needed anything to relieve the unbearable pain of empty loneliness and heartache. Nothing... but then I felt a soft nudging under my arm. A little white nose appeared. It made me laugh through the tears. Hearing me laugh, Merl responded by laying his head so gently on top of my arm. He looked into my tear-filled eyes and I could read him plain as day, *I am here for you. I love you. It will be okay.* Tears refilled my eyes. I looked at him and said, "You're such a good dog!" I wrapped my arms around him and hugged him tight. Merl hated to be confined to a hug, but somehow he seemed to know at that moment I needed to hold on to him and he endured it. He knew I was hurting and he gave me his love. I think God gave us dogs to show us just how much He loves us with that same unconditional love. I think many times they are the answer to the prayers we ask.

Because of the unconditional love that dogs give so freely, their loss can be even harder to endure than the loss of humans. Merl and Cowgirl have showered me with unconditional love when I never deserved it.

Like dogs, God calls *us* to be gentle as doves with everyone we meet and to come to Him as a child.

For a season, I worked at a real estate office on Main Street in downtown Darby, Montana. As usual, Merl was in the back of the truck. It was his truck, but I was allowed to drive it. Each day during the school year, the elementary school kids walked home past the office around 2:30. If the truck was parked on that side of the street, the children, one by one, would stop by the truck and talk to Merl. To greet them, he leaned over the bed to let them pet him and gently licked each of them on the hand or the side of their face. They loved him and he loved all people especially the kids. Once in a while, one of the kids tried to get Merl to go home with him but Merl knew his ultimate master and never crossed that line.

Merl had an unconditional love that went beyond any person I ever met. When my folks sold the ranch and moved into town, they bought a motel in Lewiston, Idaho. It looked like a motel out of the late 50's and 60's. A 'mom and pop' kind of place. They worked hard to keep it tidy and looking nice, but the truth was it was older and consequently they couldn't charge a lot for their rooms. Because of that, the clientele wasn't always the cream of the crop by society's standards. Occasionally in the wintertime one of the local churches would take pity on one of the homeless folks who were down on their luck and buy them a couple of nights in the motel to help get them cleaned up and out of the inclement weather.

One Christmas I went over to visit Mom and Dad at the Motel. Merl had his routine and every morning around 5:00 a.m. he needed to go outside and do his *dog business*. The older my dad got, the earlier he seemed to get up. Dad was already up, reading the paper and drinking coffee. After letting Merl outside to do his thing, I got a cup of coffee and sat down at the kitchen table. Hearing me sit down, dad peered over the top of the newspaper with a mischievous look in his eye. Dad loved to play cribbage and never missed an opportunity to play a game with anyone, especially if he thought he might have some sort of advantage! Seeing me sipping that first cup of coffee with hair pointing in a variety of directions and the lingering sleep in my eyes, he figured I was vulnerable.

He quickly folded the paper and set it on the chair next to him he said, "I suppose we better test the water!" with a sly grin on his face.

Never turning down a challenge, especially a cribbage game, I replied, "Pack your lunch buddy!" and the game was on.

When dad and I played cribbage, it wasn't a casual game of cards. No, each of us had our own deck, and it was marathon cribbage. Non-stop. When my Uncle Larry came over and joined in we could play all day.

Each of us had our own deck of cards and an old butter container of change set to the side. The stakes were not terribly high unless you were on a losing streak. It was a penny a point, a quarter per skunk and half dollar for a double skunk. Time evaporated when we got to playing cribbage.

Before long both Mom and the sun were up and I realized that I had left Merl outside. Normally that would not have concerned me, but we were in town and at the motel. There was a lot more traffic especially in the morning. People were getting up and in a hurry to get on the road and off to their destinations.

I opened the door and was quite surprised to see that Merl was not on the back step. My heart beat a little quicker anticipating what may have happened to him. I pulled my boots on and grabbing my coat walked out into the parking lot searching for any sign of him. I turned past the corner of the office and over on the far corner of the motel by unit fourteen, I saw him sitting next to a guy who was sitting on the step smoking a cigarette. I stopped short and watched the guy as he was talking to Merl. Merl was listening intently taking it all in. I watched the man take a long pull on his cigarette and crushed it out on the concrete step. He pet Merl's head and seemed deep in conversation so I went on around the corner and casually headed to where they were sitting. I knew that he was one of the homeless guys. Dad had mentioned that a local church had paid for a night to get him out of the cold. He had unkempt long hair. All he had on was an unbuttoned long-sleeved shirt, dirty Levi's and was barefoot. He looked like he had taken a shower earlier but had never combed his hair. *I bet he doesn't have a comb* I thought. He was the guy that people around town called "The Preacher". I was not exactly sure why because from what I had heard he didn't seem like a preacher to me. He would quote or attempt to quote the Bible but most of it was misquoted. His mind wasn't well. I remembered seeing him previously walking around town without a shirt on, even in the winter. To be honest, he unnerved me a little. He had piercing eyes, and I remembered wondering what was going on behind them. What really shocked me was that my dog was talking to him. As I walked over, Merl heard my familiar footsteps and turned to look at me, his butt wiggling a greeting. Following Merl's gaze, "The Preacher" looked up at me too. I noticed his piercing eyes were filled with tears. He quickly wiped them away nervously composing himself and gruffly said, "Is this your dog?"

"Yes" I replied. "Sorry if he is bothering you."

His voiced softened and he said, "Oh, he is just listening to me talk to God. He sure is a good dog!" while gently patting Merl's head.

"Yes, he is." I said as I motioned my head for Merl to come.

Merl responded to me and came over to my side. I knew Merl wasn't bothering him but was actually a blessing to this lonely man. As I walked back to the house I thought about how much Merl touched him. I felt terrible about how I judged the homeless man and how so many others judge homeless people. Merl had offered him the amazing gift of unconditional love. It was obvious that "The Preacher" needed a little bit of love, and I was ashamed that I didn't provide it but my dog did. What a perfect example of God's love and what He wants us to be like. As I write this, I wonder if maybe Merl's unconditional love was a portion of the Christmas gift that God gave "The Preacher" that year.

There is another saying that goes something like this "If I could only be the person that my dog thinks I am!" Dog's are so incredibly optimistic and look up to us as the most amazing people in the world even when we are not! The love that our dogs have for us is remarkable, and it is a big reason why we are drawn to them. Unconditional love is powerful. It is the kind of love that God has for us. He loved us when we were sinners not worthy of His love. But despite our faults He still loves us. Believe it or not, God is actually crazy about you! He loves you so much, and all He wants is a relationship with you!

A Bone to Chew On:

Do you feel like you love everyone unconditionally?
That's tough, isn't it?

Is it easier for you to love some people more than
others?

Are you too busy to stop and listen to what is going on
in someone else's life?

Have you ever been destitute on the street or so lonely
and wanted just anyone to talk to?

Mathew 25:34-36 *"Then shall the King say unto them on his right hand, Come, ye blessed of my Father, inherit the kingdom prepared for you from the foundation of the world:* **For I was hungry, and ye gave me meat: I was thirsty, and ye gave me drink: I was a stranger, and ye took me in; Naked, and ye clothed me: I was sick, and ye visited me: I was in prison, and ye came unto me.***"*

James 2:5-9 *Hearken, my beloved brethren, Hath not God chosen the poor of this world rich in faith, and heirs of the kingdom which he hath promised to them that love him? But ye have despised the poor. Do not rich men oppress you, and draw you before the judgment seats? Do not they blaspheme that worthy name by the which ye are called? If ye fulfil the royal law according to the scripture, Thou shalt love thy neighbour as thyself, ye do well: But if ye have respect to persons, ye commit sin, and are convinced of the law as transgressors.*

James 2: 15-16 *" If a brother or sister be naked, and destitute of daily food, And one of you say unto them, Depart in peace, be* ye *warmed and filled; notwithstanding ye give them not those things which are needful to the body; what* doth it *profit?"*

Jump!

Over the years Merl and I did a lot of hunting and fishing together. Our last hunting trip was in the steep Salmon River country of central Idaho.

Sporting a red beak and a black mask, chukar partridge thrived in that steep country. Their bright red legs could out climb any person or dog. Chukars are difficult to hunt mainly because of the steepness of the terrain, but also because they are notorious at sitting tight until you are balancing precariously on a rock with one foot, desperately searching for solid footing with the other while hanging on with a death grip to the mountainside by a handful of bitterbrush when they erupt from their cover. Surprise is their ultimate survival tactic. I believe Chukars have tactical seminars on how to avoid being shot with tactical aerial maneuvers and how to invoke heart failure using surprise tactics. If your heart survives the shock, most likely you would die from the fall induced by contorting yourself into position to get a shot. The odds of hitting a Chukar dropped dramatically in correlation to the steepness of the hillside. At my house, if I have invited guests to a dinner of Chukar they are a highly revered guest. They are that good of eating and must be for the effort taken to get them on the plate!

Merl and I were driving up the Salmon River Road going steelhead fishing when a covey of the masked birds ran across the road ahead of us. It was later in the year, and the birds were pretty skittish. They were already a good way up the hill when I pulled into a wide spot in the road. Hearing the truck door open, they all took flight again and landed further up in the draw. I grabbed my pack, a handful of shells, the shotgun, and let Merl out of the truck.

My knees ached and thighs burned with every step up the steep hill. Within five minutes of climbing, I gasped for air and stopped to wipe the sweat from my forehead that had begun to run into my eyes. I noticed that Merl was having trouble too. We were both getting old. I thought about all the hunting trips we had been on and how he had always been at my side. Suddenly out of nowhere, Chukars got up all around us. I fumbled the shotgun up to my shoulder and happened to get three shots off missing the first one by a mile, connected the second and feathers flew on the third. Merl wasted no time heading to the first bird and I kept my eye on the second bird when he set his wings and with the rest of the covey landed over on the next ridge.

Side hilling over to where Merl headed was brutal, especially through the bottom of the draw. The brush was thick but at least it gave me something to hang onto so I didn't fall off the mountain. By the time I got there Merl was standing next to the first bird. I picked it up, patted Merl's head and we headed over to where the other birds had lit on the next ridge. It took us fifteen minutes to work our way over, and I started walking the area off in a grid when a lone bird got up. I wheeled around and shot, sending it to the ground, tumbling down the steep hillside. It came to rest on a large rock in the open about seventy-five yards down the hill. It left a pretty good feather trail, and it would be easy to find.

I turned back towards Merl who was standing by a large clump of bitter brush with his ears cocked to one side looking underneath it. I said, "What? Did you find something?" He turned to me wiggled his butt and continued looking in under the bush. Walking over, I looked back under the bush, and there was the Chukar tucked deep underneath. I grabbed it and stuck it into my pack. Then we headed down the hill to where that last bird had fallen.

I told Merl what a good dog he was and how proud I was of him. The last one was easy to find and adding it to the others in my pack, we cautiously worked our way down the hill back towards the truck. Going downhill was much more difficult than going uphill. I looked at the river and the road below. If we followed the ridge down, we would come out just down the road from where the truck was parked.

The going was slow and as we picked our way down the steep hillside, I noticed that Merl too was having trouble going down the hill too. He was plumb wore out. I tried to pick the easiest trail for him. It was so steep in spots that I could not see all the way down to the road. We had been going at this for a while and eventually we came to a drop off. It was about a five-foot cliff and then continued down another twenty yards before coming out on to the road. I looked at the cliff and debated whether to try jumping off. It was a big jump, but we were almost to the road. I looked back up the hill to see where we had to go to avoid this altogether. We would have had to climb a half hour and cross over the draw the way we had come.

I looked at Merl. He just stared at the ground with his tongue hanging out, panting. I grabbed a bottle of water from my backpack and gave him a drink. He drank a lot and looked at me with thankful eyes. I asked him if he was all right; he just about fell over when he wiggled his butt. He was so tired that his legs were rubbery. We were going to have to try to go over the cliff. I unloaded my shotgun, lowered it down to some bunchgrass clumps that were growing out of the cliff, dropped my backpack below and scooted my butt to the edge. I had to jump and land just right, leaning back into the hill. If the momentum caused me to go forward, I wouldn't be able to stop and I would roll all the way down to the road. That would ruin my whole day.

Sitting at the edge, my heart was pounding loudly when I finally made the jump. The landing was in soft dirt and I sat back into the hill on impact. Perfect! I got up and grabbed my shotgun, laid it down against a rock next to me and turned to Merl. I was shocked at how far up he was and from the look on his face so was he! It was much further than I had anticipated. In fact, I couldn't even reach him! I called him and watched his eyes survey every possible scenario for a way down. Seeing none, he looked at me with the saddest look I have ever seen in that dog's eyes. I wanted to cry for him. He was scared and wanted to come to me but just couldn't do it. In that instant, I saw how old and helpless he was and it ripped my heart out. I stood on the tips of my toes stretching as far as I could for his collar but couldn't reach him. I couldn't even touch his white toes.

I stepped back and said, "Merl? You're going to have to jump!"

He looked at me in fear. His front paws moved back and forth and I thought he was going to do it. I was worried, knowing Merl I thought he might try to jump off to the side of me and get hurt rolling down the hill. I figured that when he did jump, I needed to grab his collar in midair and bring him in to the hillside where I was.

Again, I called to him. He whined and his front paws moved back and forth like he was kneading bread. He tried to muster the courage to do it. I said, "C'mon buddy, I got ya. I promise." while patting my chest.

His front paws moved back and forth, and then he jumped straight at me! Both of his front feet wrapped around my neck in a death grip. If we were going to die, we were going out together! I am not sure who was happier when I pried his legs from around my neck, but we both sat there on the side of that mountain for a couple of minutes very thankful that experience was over with!

We made it the rest of the way down easily, and as we walked back up the road towards the truck I was thinking about how scared Merl was and how difficult it was for him to trust me to catch him. That took everything he had. When he was younger there was no way that he would have jumped. It took many years for him to get to the point where he would trust me.

I think that is what this whole life experience is about. It is an opportunity to get to know the one and only Creator of the universe, day by day, every day through many trials. It takes time to build a relationship with someone and it does with God as well. He wants a relationship with you and is doing His best to get your attention if you look back on your life. Have you ever noticed how we have a knack for getting ourselves in trouble? Then we beg Him to get us out of it. Eventually we get to the point where we can trust Him with everything. For some of us, it will take our whole life before we get it. Others seem to get it right away.

You have probably been in a situation like that a time or two in your life or maybe you are there right now. From where you are standing it looks like there is no way out!

God is holding out His hands and telling you, "Jump, I've got you!" It is so hard because you cannot see Him. Sometimes it takes a traumatic experience to get us to the point where we must make that jump. Once you make that decision to trust Jesus, your life will be changed in the most amazing way that you ever dreamed possible! Give it all to Him, even that pack you have been carrying around. Drop it and make the jump.

A Bone to Chew On:

What are you carrying around in your backpack?

Have you ever been in a tight spot and the Lord asked you to "Jump"?

Do you trust Him? What scares you about that?

Do you feel like you are packing around extra weight from life's issues?

Psalm 46:1 "**God** *is* **our refuge and strength, A very** present help **in trouble**.."

Matthew 11:28-30 *"**Come to Me, all you who labor and are heavy laden, and I will give you rest**. Take My yoke upon you and learn from Me, for I am gentle and lowly in heart, and you will find rest for your souls. For **My yoke is easy and My burden is light**."*

Watch Dogs

Do you remember the classic television series *Lassie*?

Inevitably there would be a time in the show when Lassie would come running home, barking to one of the grownups . They would say something like, "What is it, girl? Is it Timmy? Timmy fell in the well over on the Johnson's place?" Then all the neighbors would get together and follow Lassie to wherever Timmy was and get him out. Lassie would save the day, which was only right; she was the star of the show. Lassie was an amazing dog, and while most of our dogs don't have that great of a vocabulary, they still let us know if danger is coming.

When Julie and I were married, we lived on a remote Forest Service compound in Montana. A large lightning storm came through the district igniting multiple forest fires. There were so many fires that the district crews couldn't handle all of them. To add to the trouble, the conditions had been very dry that year and the fires blew up and become large project fires quickly. Due to the lack of manpower and exhausted resources, the Forest Service called for recruits from other districts as far away as California, Oregon, and Alaska and sometimes even from back east.

In those days, I sketched pretty well. Some of the "Overhead Team" got wind of that and asked if I would draw up a design for the daily shift plan covers, and design a fire t-shirt for the firefighters that were on that project fire. I agreed to do it and came up with a nice pen and ink sketch of something related to that fire, put some text on it and presented it to them. They approved it so I stuck my neck out and had a hundred or so t-shirts in various colors and sizes printed. The overhead team allowed me to sell them to the firefighters as they got off their shifts in the evening.

I parked my truck near the Fire Camp. Merl was in the back of the pick-up, and I used the tailgate as my desk. I hung the shirts on hangers on the side racks of the truck, displaying the various colors and sizes that were available. A group of guys were standing around contemplating which shirts to buy and what color they wanted. I noticed Merl intently watched a guy walking up the road by himself, towards us. He looked normal enough, but I could tell that Merl was sensing something different. His hackles went up on his back and he started growling. That was a surprise to me because Merl wasn't like that. In fact, I had never seen him growl at *any* person before. When I told Merl to stop, he sat in the furthest corner of the truck with his eyes fixed on the man. When the man approached me, he stood next to the truck and stuck his hand inside the truck bed. Merl showed his teeth, growling. He started laughing at Merl. I approached him and told him to get away from the truck, if he wanted to buy a shirt then buy it and move on. I told him, "My dog doesn't trust you and neither do I". He never bought a shirt but just laughed, looked at Merl and me and walked off.

Merl was a dog I could turn loose at an ice cream social on Sunday afternoon as two-year-old children hung all over him with their ice cream cones in their hand, pulling on his hair, and he wouldn't so much as whimper. He wouldn't even eat their ice cream . . . unless it fell on the ground. Then all bets were off and it was fair game! I did not know what Merl saw in that man he didn't like, but I was going to take Merl's side on that one.

Our dogs are protective of us just like God is with His children. He gives us warnings of things that could harm us, but we need to pay attention to what He is telling us. That is why it is so important to have a solid relationship with Him so we can understand what He is saying, and act upon it quickly. We get to know Him as we read His Word, the Bible. He sent the Holy Spirit to help us after He was crucified, rose and went back to the Father. The Holy Spirit dwells in us when we take Jesus as our Savior. He is the one who talks to us in that quiet little voice. But a word of caution; we need to be careful because Satan can talk to us in a little voice as well. That is where having that *rock-solid* relationship with Jesus is so important. The longer we walk with

Him, the more we recognize God's voice. An important thing to remember is that God will *never* contradict what His Word says. That is why it is so important to be in the Bible every day. We will be able to spot when that little voice doesn't mesh with the Word of God.

One time Merl and I were hunting elk antlers in the upper Salmon River country of central Idaho. Elk dropped or shed their large antlers in late March through mid-April. The weather was always changing in the mountains so it was not unusual to get an unexpected thunderstorm in the springtime.

It was later in May and the vegetation was starting to leaf out and green up pretty good, so finding sheds was becoming increasingly difficult. I was trying to train Merl to spot the sheds, and he was getting the idea but . . . yeah, not really. He would find some bones of a winterkill and would go over and stand by them all proud of himself and, well, it's just not the same thing. I figured if I could get him trained to find sheds, we could make a killing while getting some exercise, too.

The ridges diving down to the river in the Salmon River country were very steep, especially on the sides, so the elk were confined primarily to the ridge tops. As we hiked this particular ridge, I noticed fresh elk tracks, with at least one of them being a bull. A bull's scat had an indentation on one end formed from the prostate gland and a bull also urinated in the middle of his bed whereas a cow urinated at one end of the bed. Based on the sign, I saw there was a good chance of finding an elk antler somewhere along that ridge.

Off in the distance, I heard the rumble of thunder. Looking up into the sky, I saw that it was getting darker down river. Within an hour, the thunder was louder and skies were building in intensity. The afternoon heat quickened the buildup of the storm and the skies were becoming noticeably darker and the wind had picked up rustling the treetops. I started looking for a way to get off the top of the ridge, but it was too steep to bail off just anywhere. I knew that the elk would not go off anywhere that wasn't safe; they knew that country much better than I did so I watched their tracks. The storm closed in more quickly than I had anticipated. Time was running out. I smelled rain in the air. Merl sensed it too and whined. Flashes of lightning were becoming more common now and the echo of thunder rattled repeatedly down the canyon walls. A tree in front of me caught my attention. It had a distinct spiraling scar down its bark, the definitive sign of a lightning strike. I looked at other trees on the ridge; several of them had been hit by lightning in the past. There must have been some mineral in the rock on this ridge that made this a hot spot.

I felt like a lightning rod with the backpack frame on my back. Quickening my pace, my eyes searched frantically for a place to bail off the ridge. Merl refrained from sniffing every bush and stayed closer to me sensing my urgency. Lightning and thunder didn't spook Merl like it

143

did some dogs, but I could tell he was getting a little anxious too. Suddenly a flash of lightning lit up the sky just beyond the ridge we were on. I counted. *One, one thousand, two, one thous* . . . and BOOMMM! Thunder rattled down the canyon. I looked at Merl and he got closer still, looking up at me. I noticed that his ears were back a little. That one got his attention, and mine too. I said, "Yeah, I know. We need to get off this ridge!" He let out another whine. I picked up the pace, and he ran ahead of me and then cut off to the side looking back at me. I saw disturbed soil in the hillside where a small herd of elk had run off down the side hill. We were running out of time and needed to get off the ridge soon!

"Good dog!" I said.

Merl sensed my agreement and cautiously headed off the ridge, following the elk tracks down the steep hillside. The decomposed granite gave way, dramatically overextending every step. A cold raindrop hit my arm. It was a big one. The sky was dark and menacing and the wind complemented it. The giant ponderosas swayed reluctantly giving way to the strong gusts coming up the canyon. Clusters of long needles torn from the limbs spiraled to the ground. I heard large raindrops hitting all around us, like bullets tearing up the loose soil with each impact.

My heartbeat gradually returned to normal and the adrenaline rush subsided as we dropped below the ridgeline. Merl stopped and looked at me when we came to a well-established game trail. We were side hilling about a quarter of the way below the ridge. I said, "Yeah, let's go back to the truck." He knew what "truck" meant and liked that idea a lot! I was just thankful to be off the top of that ridge and got lost in thought about all those spiraled trees. Walking on the game trail was much easier than side hilling in the decomposed granite. Rain was coming down steady in large drops, and I accepted the fact that we were going to get drenched. Merl stopped next to the base of a large tree, and I noticed his ears were back a bit. I came up to him and stopped next to a large ponderosa pine tree. Suddenly I felt a static charge and a white flash illuminated everything around me in a brilliant, blinding white light. Instinctively Merl and I both ducked, and I hit my knees. The ground shook with intensity as the tree on the ridge that was struck disintegrated in a split second. A large chunk of pine tree the size of my pack flew past the tree right in front of me. Another one hit the giant ponderosa I had just walked behind taking the blow. The sound was deafening and simultaneous with the flash. My heart raced as I sat on my knees listening to the thunder echo off the canyon walls and fade into nothing but raindrops.

I looked at the chunk of pine lying on the ground in front of me. It was the size of a camp cooler. If that giant ponderosa tree would not have been there I would be walking around without a head! It felt like all

145

my wet hair was standing straight out, my hands and knees were shaking. Merl came up and leaned into me. He was shaking too.

Whether it's the UPS man or something traumatic, our dogs give us warnings when they see things coming. Some dogs are better at reading signs than others, and those are the watchdogs. Like those watchdogs, there are some people who are called to be watchdogs, or "watchmen." God has called them to give a warning to the rest of His people when they see things start to happen. God sent prophets to warn people about what was coming, and they wrote it down in the Bible.

Did you know that a third of the Bible is prophetic? You see, God loves us so much that He tries everything possible to get us to open our eyes to establish a relationship with Him. We all have a choice whether to listen to these "watchmen" or not. God has always given His people a warning before He did something. He is very patient and He does not want to see anyone perish, but the truth of the matter is, there is only a certain allotment of time set aside for this age of grace that we are in. When the time is up, the whistle is going to blow and it will be, "Everybody out of the pool!"

Noah preached for hundreds of years to people and no one listened to him. They all laughed at him and mocked him when he was building his ark. One day Noah and his family got on the ark six days before it started raining. Everyone outside the ark laughed at him, but in the end, they all drowned.

Whoa! Did you just feel a raindrop? It was a big one!

A Bone to Chew On:

Are you paying attention to how prophecy in the Bible is matching what is going on in the world today?

What signs do you see and hear?

Can you see the storm that is rapidly coming up the canyon?

Ezekiel 3:17-19 *Son of man, I have made thee a watchman unto the house of Israel: therefore hear the word at my mouth, and give them warning from me. When I say unto the wicked, Thou shalt surely die; and thou givest him not warning, nor speakest to warn the wicked from his wicked way, to save his life; the same wicked* man *shall die in his iniquity; but his blood will I require at thine hand._Yet if thou warn the wicked, and he turn not from his wickedness, nor from his wicked way, he shall die in his iniquity; but thou hast delivered thy soul.*

Revelation 1:3 "***Blessed* is *he** who reads and those who hear the words of this prophecy, and keep those things which are written in it; for the time* is *near."*

Acknowledgments

To God's inspiration and His prompting to write this book. I appreciate His gift of creativity and vision. To Him goes ALL the Glory!

Obviously none of this would have been written without my two dogs. For both of them I am so grateful! What a blessing both of them have been! Merl has passed on and probably has a cat treed at the entrance to Heaven while waiting for me and Cowgirl to get there. Cowgirl is at my side patiently waiting for me to stop writing so we can go for a ride in the truck! And.... Frank. His story is on-going. Like so many of us, his story is huge, especially for such a short dog.

Karen Simmons, who, with her patience, has endured this process every day with me. Her encouragement is amazing and she is truly a blessing and I am so thankful for her.

Deb Allen was so helpful to me through the writing process. Her encouragement was a great addition to this book.

Noelle Stebbins and her inspired wisdom on the free will God has given us. She is a good friend.

Kelley MacQuain, Brenda Mahler and Sandy Wilson with their talents in editing this book.

This and other books written by William H. Cox can be purchased at

www.rustyironranchllc.com

Made in the USA
Columbia, SC
13 November 2018